Building Community
in Schools

Thomas J. Sergiovanni

Building Community
in Schools

Jossey-Bass Publishers · San Francisco

Substantial discounts on bulk quantities of Jossey-Bass books are available to corporations, professional associations, and other organizations. For details and discount information, contact the special sales department at Jossey-Bass Inc., Publishers. (415) 433-1740; Fax (415) 433-0499.

For sales outside the United States, contact Maxwell Macmillan International Publishing Group, 866 Third Avenue, New York, New York 10022.

Manufactured in the United States of America

 The paper used in this book is acid-free and meets the State of California requirements for recycled paper (50 percent recycled waste, including 10 percent postconsumer waste), which are the strictest guidelines for recycled paper currently in use in the United States.

10% POST CONSUMER WASTE

The ink in this book is either soy- or vegetable-based and during the printing process emits fewer than half the volatile organic compounds (VOCs) emitted by petroleum-based ink.

Library of Congress Cataloging-in-Publication Data

Sergiovanni, Thomas J.
  Building community in schools / Thomas J. Sergiovanni. — 1st ed.
    p.   cm. — (The Jossey-Bass education series)
  Includes bibliographical references (p.   ) and index.
  ISBN 1-55542-571-2 (alk. paper)
    1. School management and organization—United States.
  2. Interpersonal relations.   3. Organizational behavior—United
  States.   4. Schools—United States—Sociological aspects.
  5. Educational change—United States.   6. Community and school
  —United States.   I. Title.   II. Series.
  LB2805.S518   1993
  371.2'00973—dc20   93-19582
                                                               CIP

Credits are on page 221.

FIRST EDITION
HB Printing   10 9 8 7 6 5 4 3 2 1   *Code 9367*

*The Jossey-Bass
Education Series*

Contents

Preface

The story I tell in *Building Community in Schools* is a simple one. Though most principals, superintendents, and teachers have a desire to do better and are working as hard as they can to provide a quality education to every student they serve, the road is rough and the going is slow. The lead villain in this frustrating drama is the loss of community in our schools and in society itself. If we want to rewrite the script to enable good schools to flourish, we need to rebuild community. Community building must become the heart of any school improvement effort. Whatever else is involved—improving teaching, developing sensible curriculum, creating new forms of governance, providing more authentic assessment, empowering teachers and parents, increasing professionalism—it must rest on a foundation of community building.

"Community?" you might respond. "What's new about that? We're already into community." Clearly "community" is the new buzzword in the language of education. Yesterday it was "culture" rivaled by "empowerment," "collegiality," and "transformational." The day before it was "MBO," "situational leadership," "school effectiveness," and "instructional leadership." Yesterday's ideas are still popular but are beginning to slip a little. These ideas are on the wane.

Allan Kennedy, coauthor of *Corporate Cultures*, was giving a talk to a group of executives. After his presentation one executive remarked, "This corporate culture stuff is great," then turned to one of his subordinates and said, "I want a culture by

Monday morning." Like that executive, we are all a little guilty of
seeking quick fixes. We are prone to march off to those three
days of training in search of the silver bullet that will transform
us and our schools. But the Monday mornings come and go with
little effect in the long run.

Let's face it, the field of education is prone to faddism.
Most school people care a great deal about what they do and
want things to be better. We want so much to succeed that easy
answers and canned solutions hold out tantalizing promises.
Those who propose quick fixes are expert at capitalizing on our
vulnerability, as a quick review of advertisements in the popular
educational press will testify.

The ideas behind the fads are often very useful and promising for improving things. A good idea becomes a fad when it is
adopted and used at the level of practice without a change at the
level of theory. Reducing good ideas to prescriptions is an example. When we do this we commit an epistemological error that
plagues the school reform movement. Epistemological errors
are not scientific errors but errors in perspective. And because
they are not scientific errors, they are typically overlooked. Thus
we keep on making the same errors over and over again by
introducing new practices, even though they seem not to affect
anything very much or for very long.

Changing the basic theory of schooling means changing
how we think and what we believe. This kind of change, according to John Weins (1992), superintendent of the Seven Oaks
Schools in Winnipeg, Manitoba, requires a rethinking of our
most common, entrenched, and fundamental educational beliefs, structures, practices, and behaviors. Weins is working with
other Seven Oaks administrators who make up the superintendents' team in an effort to redefine the superintendency itself.
"We needed to first change the superintendency before we had a
right to request others in the system to entertain or consider
change—it was the least we had to do; it might be the most we
could do" (p. 3). He notes further, "The Superintendents' Team,
collectively and individually, attempt to be *educational leaders*
first, in whatever they do. This means that we must be *teachers* in
everything we do—our directions must reflect educational pur-

poses and our actions must be pedagogical and educative"
(p. 47). Weins believes that adopting a new theory for Seven
Oaks requires reframing administrative questions into educational terms, inventing new systems of authority and accountability and new ways of providing recognition and rewards, and
rethinking educational purposes and practices. If Seven Oaks is
successful in changing its basic theory of knowing and doing,
then it will be successful in creating a new practice of schooling.

Given these observations, I would respond to claims that
"we're already into community" by asking whether we are into
authentic community or counterfeit community. Authentic community requires us to do more than pepper our language with
the word "community," label ourselves as a community in our
mission statement, and organize teachers into teams and
schools into families. It requires us to think community, believe
in community, and practice community—to change the basic
metaphor for the school itself to community. We are into authentic community when community becomes embodied in the
school's policy structure itself, when community values are at the
center of our thinking.

Need for Community

Why is community building important in schools? Community
is the tie that binds students and teachers together in special
ways, to something more significant than themselves: shared
values and ideals. It lifts both teachers and students to higher
levels of self-understanding, commitment, and performance—
beyond the reaches of the shortcomings and difficulties they
face in their everyday lives. Community can help teachers and
students be transformed from a collection of "I's" to a collective
"we," thus providing them with a unique and enduring sense of
identity, belonging, and place.

The need for community is universal. A sense of belonging, of continuity, of being connected to others and to ideas and
values that make our lives meaningful and significant—these
needs are shared by all of us. Their loss, for whatever reason,
requires us to search for substitutes, which are not always func-

tional. Loss of community, for example, is manifested in the large number of troubled families now acknowledged to exist in the United States and Canada.

At an earlier time in our history, much of the socialization of our young people was shared. Families counted, but so did the extended family and the neighborhood. This life-style embodied the popular African proverb, "It takes a village to raise a child." Today we are experiencing a loss of community in the extended family and in the "village" too. The neighborhood lives of young people are often disconnected from society and sometimes even alienated, forcing them to turn inward and to rely on themselves for support. But membership always has a price. If you want to belong, you have to believe. Unfortunately the norms and systems that evolve—and to which young people adhere as they search for community on their own—are often dysfunctional.

One solution to the problem of dysfunctional substitutes for community is to provide substitutes for the substitutes. For example, if gangs substitute for family and neighborhood by providing students with the sense of community that they need, then schools must create substitutes for gangs by providing an alternative sense of community that makes more sense to students. When the student subculture is beyond the reach of adult influence, we might consider it "wild" as opposed to "domesticated." Community building is the secret weapon that can help domesticate the wild cultures that now seem so omnipresent in our schools.

I do not believe that authentic community is rare in schools. Indeed there are many wonderful books that describe schools that embody community in how they organize and in what they do. George Wood's *Schools That Work* (1992) and Edward Fiske's *Smart Schools, Smart Kids* (1991) are two recent examples. The celebrated Central Park East Secondary School in New York City and the Network of Secondary Schools in Cologne, Germany (Köln-Holweide is the best known), are frequently cited as models of community. Many other lesser-known examples abound.

We need now to go beyond the descriptive to the conceptual if we want to facilitate the spread of community building in our schools. From the celebrated models and from other images of schools that embody community, I draw the thoughts and concepts that, as common threads, can provide an idea struc- ture, a mental armature, a set of theoretical frames to help parents, principals, teachers, and students discover community for themselves and to create community in their own schools. Further, I recast the concept of community into the language of mainstream education by exploring the implications of commu- nity for how teaching and learning should be understood and practiced as well as for how we should inquire into the curricu- lum and decide what is worth teaching and learning. The recon- ceptualization of community can help us grapple with a host of other perennially important issues such as assessment, disci- pline, school organization, teachers' workplace, climate, and leadership.

Successful community building depends in a large mea- sure on each individual school defining for itself its own life and creating for itself its own practice of schooling. This inside-out strategy requires a considerable amount of searching and reflec- tion as teachers struggle with such issues as who they are, what they hope to become for the students they serve, and how they will decide, organize, teach, learn, and live together.

Overview

In this book, I seek to provide a view of community that teachers and principals can use to think about what community means to them and to struggle together to build community in their schools.

Chapter One critiques the traditional view of schools as formal organizations, pointing out that this view fails both students and teachers, no matter how good our intentions. A prime reason for this failure is the inability of schools to help students recover the loss of community that too many now experience. I then offer a theory of community as an alternative. This theory can help schools become places where relationships are familylike, where space and time resemble a neighborhood, and where a code of values and ideas is shared. This theory, in other words, can help schools become communities by kinship—of place and of mind. Changing our theory of schooling from organization to community does not require a massive restructuring of schools, but it does require that we think and behave differently.

Political scientists, sociologists, psychologists, and theologians all use the word *community* but mean different things by it. For our purposes I offer the following definition of community: communities are collections of individuals who are bonded together by natural will and who are together binded to a set of shared ideas and ideals. This bonding and binding is tight enough to transform them from a collection of "I's" into a collective "we." As a "we," members are part of a tightly knit web of meaningful relationships. This "we" usually shares a common place and over time comes to share common sentiments and traditions that are sustaining. When describing community it is helpful to speak of community by kinship, of mind, of place, and of memory.

In Chapter Two I point out that though community may exist in many forms, the quality of relationships that administrators, teachers, and students experience is key. Relationships in communities are characterized by the kinds of emotions—personalization, authenticity, caring, and unconditional acceptance—found in families, extended families, neighborhoods, and other social organizations. Relying on school examples, recent research on the importance of relationships within schools in leveraging change, and the seminal work of Talcott Parsons and Mary Rousseau, I describe a pattern of relationships characteristic of communities. This pattern is then used to help those interested in community building to evaluate the quality of relationships that exist among teachers, between teachers and schools, and between administrators and teachers.

Many schools are now deeply involved in community building. In Chapter Three I provide examples of community by kinship, community of place, and community of mind by describing community building at New York's Central Park East Secondary School and at the Köln-Holweide School in Cologne,

Germany. Both are celebrated examples frequently cited in the media and the literature, and both lay the groundwork for discussions of other facets of community building that appear in subsequent chapters. The Denali School in Fairbanks, Alaska, and the Jackson-Keller School in San Antonio, Texas, less celebrated but equally worthy examples of community building, are discussed in later chapters.

Chapter Four discusses our need for community and why, once community is offered, we willingly accept it. We humans, it is argued, respond to both rational and cultural connections between us and our wants, among us, and between us and our work. Rational connections emphasize the "I" and are manifested in individual quests for satisfaction of our own self-interests. Cultural connections, by contrast, are embedded in the norms, customs, and mores that tie us to others who share common conceptions. It is the cultural connections in a school that bond principals, students, and teachers together into a "we." Whether one looks to contemporary needs theories or to our anthropological history as a human species, it becomes clear that the potential for becoming a "we" is stronger than the propensity to remain an "I." In schools, when this potential is frustrated, students turn elsewhere for substitutes, building community among themselves with often dysfunctional results.

The theme of Chapter Five is becoming a purposeful community. Schools, for example, can become caring communities where members make a total commitment to each other; learning communities where learning is an attitude as well as an activity; professional communities where the ideals of professional virtue flourish; collegial communities where members are tied together by a sense of felt interdependence and mutual obligation; inclusive communities where differences are brought together into a mutually respectful whole; and inquiring communities where members commit themselves to a spirit of collective inquiry. But to be any of these, schools must first become purposeful communities. They must become places where members have developed a community of mind that bonds them together in a special way and binds them to a shared

ideology. The quest to become a purposeful community is illustrated by case studies and other school examples.

In Chapter Six emphasis is given to how shared purposes
and values are translated into decisions about what should be
taught in schools and how the curriculum should be organized.
Key to this effort is providing enough structure and direction to
enable a shared community of mind to emerge that shapes what
goes on in the community while at the same time allowing
enough discretion for the school to function as a professional
community. Both discipline and discretion are needed to make
community work.

Chapter Seven shows how the power of community can be
used to help transform present discipline policies and classroom management practices that emphasize control over what
students do into community strategies that help build moral
character and teach active citizenship. Schools have an obligation to teach citizenship and to develop caring adults, and the
best way to teach these values is by actually living them. The
dominant themes in leading a democratic life are obligations
and duties, not rights and freedoms. These themes provide the
rationale for schools and classrooms to become democratic
communities.

The meaning of professional community is the theme of
Chapter Eight. Instead of looking inward to teaching, we have
imported the meaning of professionalism from other fields.
Borrowed conceptions encourage us to view professionalism as
a technical activity involving the delivery of expert services to
clients. As a result, we tend to think of professionalism in teaching exclusively along themes of expertness, thus neglecting professional virtue, which is at the core of what it means to be a
professional community. This chapter defines and discusses
professional virtue.

Building a community of learners is explored in Chapter
Nine. As principals and teachers inquire together they create
community. Becoming a community of learners is an adventure
not only in learning but in shared leadership and in authentic
relationships. The example of Denali School in Fairbanks,
Alaska, shows what happens when a school accepts the chal-

lenge to become a community of learners. This is a story of an emotional and intellectual awakening that transformed principal, teachers, parents, and students.

Chapter Ten discusses what is involved when a school becomes a community of leaders. Learning together makes sense to most of us, but leading together defies some of the norms of leadership we have been taught and have come to accept. Most of us believe that no matter how progressive leadership is expressed, underneath it is still something that individual leaders do in an effort to influence what others think and do. In communities, by contrast, leadership is redefined. The emphasis, for example, is no longer on "power over" others but on "power to" accomplish shared visions and goals. And in communities, the obligations to lead are shared by everyone. The school becomes a community of leaders. This transformation is illustrated by the story of the Jackson-Keller School in San Antonio, Texas—a story of struggle and discovery as principal and teachers together became a community of leaders.

In Chapter Eleven leadership itself is redefined. Though its instrumental qualities remain important, the heart of leadership in community is not so much doing but being. Through being, leaders plant the seeds of community, nurture fledgling community, and protect the community once it emerges. They lead by following. They lead by serving. They lead by inviting others to share in the burdens of leadership. Like Plato's Guardians, they lead by knowing and they lead by being.

Audience

My intent was to write a short book that would have something useful to say to principals, teachers, superintendents, and others interested in building community. I do not write for the fainthearted, for community building takes courage. If the process is to succeed, people must be willing to change their basic ideas about schooling and about relationships within schools, and that is never easy. Nor do I provide a recipe for others to follow. Community building is a quest that requires the principal, teachers, parents, and students of each individual school to come to grips with what community means to them and to chart together the path they will follow. The theory of community I provide and the examples of community building that illustrate this theory will, I hope, help by pointing the way.

I write also for scholars in educational administration and particularly for organizational theorists. I ask them to ponder whether the very theory of organizations that gives birth to today's schools and life within them needs to be changed if schools are to improve significantly. And I invite them to consider the possibility that we might better understand schools as social rather than formal organizations and, in particular, as communities.

Acknowledgments

In *Building Community in Schools* I tell the story of countless teachers and principals who struggle every day to build community in their schools.This book is in every way their story, and I am grateful for both their struggle and for what I have learned as a result. In particular I want to thank Trinity University colleagues Shari Albright, Chula Boyle, Margaret Burns, David Flinders, John Moore, and Rose Rudnitski (now at State University of New York, New Paltz) for their insights and support. Many principals, teachers, and other school people helped, too many for me to mention individually. The contributions of David Hagstrom, Herb Rosenfeld, and Alicia Thomas were so significant, however, that they must be mentioned.

A number of anecdotes included in this book are not referenced. They were contributed by principals, superintendents, and others as part of my ongoing research on school leadership. To all, I am deeply grateful for what you have taught me about the meaning of community.

San Antonio, Texas   Thomas J. Sergiovanni
July 1993

The Author

Thomas J. Sergiovanni is Lillian Radford Professor of Education at Trinity University, San Antonio, Texas. He received his B.S. degree (1958) in elementary education from the State University of New York, College at Geneseo, his M.A. degree (1959) in educational administration from Teachers College, Columbia University, and his Ed.D. degree (1966), also in educational administration, from the University of Rochester.

From 1958 to 1964, he was an elementary school teacher and science consultant in New York State and taught in the teacher education program at the State University of New York, College at Buffalo. In 1966, he began nineteen years of service on the faculty of educational administration at the University of Illinois, Urbana-Champaign, where he chaired the department for seven years.

At Trinity University, Sergiovanni teaches in the school leadership program and in the five-year teacher education program. He is senior fellow at the Center for Educational Leadership and a founder of the Trinity Principals' Center. A former associate editor of *Educational Administration Quarterly*, he serves on the editorial boards of the *Journal of Educational Research*, the *Journal of Curriculum and Supervision*, the *Journal of Personnel Evaluation in Education*, and *Teaching Education*. Among his recent books are *Value-Added Leadership: How to Get Extraordinary Performance in Schools* (1990), *The Principalship: A Reflective Practice Perspective* (1991, 2nd ed.), and *Moral Leadership* (1992).

Building Community
in Schools

1

Changing Our
Theory of Schooling

Irwin Blumer, school superintendent in Newton, Massachusetts, neatly captures the complexities involved in creating real change: "Much of what passes for school reform is superficial and ultimately fails because the difficulty of the task — institutional change — is underestimated. Real change can only come as a result of the commitments of both the minds and hearts of the total school community — teachers, parents, students, administrators and school boards. Reform should be based on careful identification of deeply and commonly held values. Change can only be achieved through people's acceptance of responsibility to further their goals through their words and their actions" (1992, p. 1). To Blumer, commitment of the mind and heart are key if we want sustained changes in our school practices. The mind and heart represent our accepted understandings and beliefs of how the world works. These understandings and beliefs function as theories of practice that first determine and then affirm what we do.

Changing our minds is always tough because of this strong connection between doing and affirmation. Current school practices have been continuously reinforced by the existing theory. As a result, their acceptance has become so automatic that they are considered to be unquestioned truths. Things are done in a certain way because they are supposed to be done that way.

To change, we have to challenge practices that have always appeared sensible, and this is hard to do. A good place to start is

1

examining the unstated assumptions behind accepted practices. Why are teachers evaluated by supervisors at the next
higher level, who are in turn evaluated by higher-level supervisors? Why does someone at the central office have to sign off
on the purchase of first-grade books? Is it because administrators at the next higher level are more knowledgeable about
schooling and more likely to behave responsibly than those
lower? Does hierarchy, in other words, equal expertise? Does
hierarchy equal superior moral responsibility? Must clear lines
of authority be maintained and must clear responsibilities be
delineated to keep schools from losing control and avoiding
accountability?

The practices described in these examples have become
habits of the mind and heart that make sense as long as the
theory underlying schooling remains the same. Change the
theory and we will need to learn new habits. If we can get
the theory right, the right practices will follow.

We have been taught to think of schools as formal organizations and behavior within them as organizational behavior.
This forces us to think about schools in a certain way. To "organize" means to arrange things into a coherent whole. First there
has to be a reason for organizing. Then all the parts to be
organized are studied and mentally grouped into some kind of
logical order. Next, a plan is developed that enables the elements
to be arranged according to the desired scheme. Typically this is
a linear process. As the plan is being followed, progress is moni-
tored and corrections made. Finally, when the work is completed, the organizational arrangements are evaluated in terms
of original intentions. These principles seem to apply whether
we are thinking about organizing our bureau drawers or our
schools.

Schools must be considered legitimate in the eyes of their
relevant publics. Formal organizations seek legitimacy by ap-
pearing "rational." The sociologist John Meyer (1984) points out
that schools as formal organizations must develop explicit management structures and procedures that give a convincing account that the proper means-end chains are in place to accomplish stated purposes. Organizing schools into departments and

grade levels, developing job descriptions, constructing curriculum plans, and putting into place explicit instructional delivery systems of various kinds are all examples of attempts to communicate that the school knows what it's doing. Further, school administrators must convince everyone that they are in control. They do this by using rules and regulations, monitoring and supervising teachers, and other regulatory means. Teachers, in turn, develop similar schemes in efforts to control students.

Though initially organizations are creatures of people, they tend over time to become separated from people and to function independently in pursuit of their own goals and purposes. This separation has to be bridged somehow. Ties have to exist that connect people to their work and to the people they work with. In organizations the ties that connect us to others and to our work are contractual. Each person, acting separately, negotiates a settlement with others and with the organization that meets her or his needs.

Self-interest is assumed to be the prime motivation in these negotiations. Thus, for schools to get teachers to do what needs to be done, rewards must be traded for compliance. Teachers who teach the way they are supposed to get good evaluations. Good evaluations lead to better assignments and improved prospects for promotion. Bad evaluations lead to poor assignments and banishment. Teachers who cooperate get recognition, are in on the school's information system, and get picked to attend workshops and conferences. A similar pattern of rewards and punishments characterizes life within classrooms and the broader relationships that exist between students and schools.

Management and leadership are very important in schools understood as formal organizations. Since motivation comes from the outside, someone has to propose and monitor the various trades that are needed. In the classroom it is the teacher and in the school it is the principal who has this job. Both are overworked as a result. Leadership inevitably takes the form of bartering. "Leader and led strike a bargain within which the leader gives to led something they want in exchange for something the leader wants" (Sergiovanni, 1990, p. 30). Students and teachers become connected to their work for calculated reasons. Students study hard as long as they get desired rewards. Teachers go the extra mile for the same reason. When rewards are reduced or no longer desired, both give less effort.

The Community Metaphor

Not all groupings of individuals, however, can be characterized as formal organizations. Families, communities, friendship networks, and social clubs are examples of organized collections of people that are different. If we view schools as communities rather than organizations, the practices that make sense in schools understood as organizations just don't fit.

In communities, for example, the connection of people to purpose and the connections among people are not based on contracts but commitments. Communities are socially organized around relationships and the felt interdependencies that nurture them (Blau and Scott, 1962). Instead of being tied together and tied to purposes by bartering arrangements, this social structure bonds people together in a oneness and binds them to an idea structure. The bonding together of people in special ways and the binding of them to shared values and ideas are the defining characteristics of schools as communities. Communities are defined by their centers of values, sentiments, and beliefs that provide the needed conditions for creating a sense of "we" from "I."

Life in organizations and life in communities are different in both quality and kind. In communities we create our social lives with others who have intentions similar to ours. In organizations relationships are constructed for us by others and become codified into a system of hierarchies, roles, and role expectations. Communities too are confronted with issues of control. But instead of relying on external control measures communities rely more on norms, purposes, values, professional socialization, collegiality, and natural interdependence. Once established, the ties of community in schools can become substitutes for formal systems of supervision, evaluation, and staff development; for management and organizational schemes that seek to coordinate what teachers do and how they work together; and for leadership itself (Sergiovanni, 1992).

The ties also redefine how certain ideas are to be understood. With community in place, for example, empowerment of teachers, students, and others focuses less on discretion and freedom per se and more on commitment, obligations, and duties that people share together. And collegiality results less from organizational arrangements that force people to work together and from other external sources, and more from within. Community members connect with each other as a result of felt interdependencies, mutual obligations, and other ties.

A Theory of Community

There is no recipe for community building—no correlates, no workshop agenda, no training package. Community cannot be borrowed or bought.

This reality makes the job of building community harder on the one hand but better on the other. Recipes are *too easy* to implement and for that reason they too often result in practices that are grafted onto the school without significantly influencing the school for very long. If we are interested in community building, then we, along with other members of the proposed community, are going to have to invent our own practice of community. It is as simple, and as hard, as that. Despite the difficulties, if we are successful, our community will be not counterfeit but real.

Inventing a practice of community does not mean that we need to start from scratch. Theories of community exist that can help us. They can provide us with ideas and serve as a mental and emotional scaffold to help anchor our thoughts and transform them into a framework for community building.

One "theory" that can help is known as *gemeinschaft* and *gesellschaft*. I know that the use of foreign words may seem both pretentious and distant on the surface. But *gemeinschaft* and *gesellschaft* are special words that communicate a set of concepts and ideas considered seminal in sociology. The meanings they communicate are too important to risk being watered down by less exact but more familiar synonyms. When a sociologist observes that one group of individuals, one village, or one school is more *gemeinschaft* than another, or laments the loss of *gemeinschaft* in favor of *gesellschaft*, those familiar with the terms have a comprehensive and detailed image of just what is meant. The words are metaphors that bring to mind two "ideal types," two different ways of thinking and living, two alternative visions of life.

　　Gemeinschaft translates to "community" and *gesellschaft* translates to "society." The terms are attributed to the German sociologist Ferdinand Tönnies. Writing in 1887, he used the terms to describe the shifting values and orientations that occurred as we moved first from a hunting and gathering society to an agricultural society, and then on to an industrial society. Each of the societal transformations resulted in a shift away from *gemeinschaft* toward *gesellschaft*; away from a vision of life as sacred community and toward a more secular society.

Gemeinschaft

Gemeinschaft, according to Tönnies, exists in three forms: *gemeinschaft* by kinship, of place, and of mind ([1887] 1957, 42). *Gemeinschaft* by kinship comes from the unity of being, in the sense of a "we" identity that families and extended families provide. *Gemeinschaft* of place emerges from the sharing of a common habitat or locale: this is my class, my school, my neighborhood, my town, my country. As a result of this common membership and this sense of belonging, my being is enlarged from "I" to "we." *Gemeinschaft* of mind refers to the bonding together of people that results from their mutual binding to a common goal, shared set of values, and shared conception of being. *Gemeinschaft* of mind further strengthens the "we" identity. Though all three are helpful, *gemeinschaft* of mind is essential to building community within schools. As Tönnies explains, "*Gemeinschaft* of mind expresses the community of mental life. In conjunction with the others, this last type of *gemeinschaft* represents the truly human and supreme form of community" (p. 42).

As we seek to build community in all three of its forms, we might ask: What can be done to increase the sense of kinship, neighborliness, and collegiality among the faculty? How can we become more of a professional community where we care about each other and help each other to be and to learn, and to lead more productive work lives? What kind of relationships need to be cultivated with parents that will enable them to be included in our emerging community? How can we help each other? How can we redefine the web of relationships that exist among us and between us and students so that they embody community? How can we arrange our teaching and learning settings so that they are more familylike? How can the school itself, as a collection of families, become more like a neighborhood? What are the shared values and commitments that enable the school to become a community of the mind? How will these values and commitments become practical standards that can guide how we lead our lives, what we learn and how, and how we treat each other? What patterns of mutual obligations and duties emerge as community is achieved?

As these questions are answered the school begins the process of transformation from an organized collection of individuals to a community of the mind. Relationships within a community of mind are based not on contracts but on understandings about what is shared and on the emerging web of obligations to embody that which is shared. Relationships within a community by kinship are based not on contracts but on understandings similar to those found within the family. Relationships within communities of place are based not on contracts but on understandings about how members will live their lives together as neighbors.

Throughout this book I make frequent references to the family in illustrating how the theory of *gemeinschaft* can be applied to schools. Following the lead of Rev. James Close and James Wilbur (1992–1993), as they introduce "Intercessions for Holy Family Day," I use the term in its broadest sense. In their words, "The terms 'family' and 'household' have broadened in meaning beyond the usual intimate sense of spouses and children. In a conscious expression of this awareness, today's prayer of the faithful reminds us that there are also one-parent families, blended families, individuals living alone, the parish family, the community, the nation, the family of nations, and the household of faith" (p. 79).

Though not cast in stone, community understandings have enduring qualities. They are resilient enough to survive the passage of members through the community over time. They are taught to new members, celebrated in customs and rituals, and embodied as standards that govern life in the community. Enduring understandings suggests a fourth form of community— community of memory (Bellah and others, 1985). In time, communities by kinship, of place, and of mind become communities of memory.

The relationships among the four forms of community are mutually reinforcing. The connections that emerge among people from familylike feelings and relationships and from sharing a common place contribute to the development of shared values and ideas. And this community of the mind provides the basis for solidifying the feelings and identities associated with being a community of kinship and a community of place. "Whenever human beings are related through their wills in an organic manner and affirm each other we find one or another of the three types of *gemeinschaft*" (Tönnies, [1887] 1957, p. 42).

Gesellschaft

Tönnies's basic argument is that as modern society advances, the world drifts further and further away from *gemeinschaft* to *gesellschaft*. Community values are replaced by contractual ones. Secondary-group relationships come to dominate primary-group relationships (Cooley, [1909] 1956). Society becomes less sacred and more secular (Becker, 1950). Life becomes more impersonal. Connections among people and between them and their institutions become more contrived. Meaning and significance in life become more difficult to find. "The theory of *gesellschaft* deals with the artificial construction of an aggregate of human beings which superficially resemble the *gemeinschaft* insofar as the individuals live and dwell together peacefully.

However, in the *gemeinschaft* they remain essentially united in spite of all separating factors, whereas in the *gesellschaft* they are essentially separated in spite of all the uniting factors" (Tönnies, [1887] 1957, p. 64).

The cultural ramifications of *gesellschaft* are often accompanied by psychological ones. Loneliness, isolation, and feelings of being disconnected from others and from society itself are the ones most frequently mentioned (Durkheim, [1897] 1951; Seeman, 1959). Getting ahead in a *gesellschaft* world is an individual endeavor; it emphasizes mastery of a set of instrumental skills that enables one to make the right transactions in an impersonal and competitive world. "In *gesellschaft* every person strives for that which is to his own advantage as he affirms the actions of others only insofar as and as long as they can further his interests. . . all agreements of the will stand out as so many treaties and peace pacts" (Tönnies, [1887] 1957, p. 77).

Relationships in *gesellschaft* are contractual. This contrived exchange of sentiments, material wants and needs, sweat and toil, and even love itself reaches deep into all aspects of conventional life. In Tönnies's words, "Its [*gesellschaft*] supreme rule is politeness. It consists of an exchange of words and courtesies in which everyone seems to be present for the good of everyone else and everyone seems to consider everyone else as his equal, whereas in reality everyone is thinking of himself and trying to bring to the fore his importance and advantages in competition with the others" ([1887] 1957, p. 78). Tönnies refers to these exchanges as "formless contracts."

Tönnies distinguishes between natural will and rational will in explaining the basis of relationships between and among people. Social relationships, for example, don't just happen but are willed. People associate with each other for reasons. In *gemeinschaft*, natural will is the prime motivating force. People relate to each other because doing so has its own intrinsic meaning and significance. There is no tangible goal or benefit in mind for any of the parties to the relationship. In *gesellschaft*, rational will is the prime motivating force. People relate to each other to reach some goal, to gain some benefit. Without this benefit the relationship ends. In the first instance the ties among people are thick and laden with symbolic meanings. They are moral ties. In the second instance the ties among people are thin and instrumental. They are calculated ties.

The modern Western corporation is an example of *gesellschaft*. In the corporation, relationships are formal and distant, having been prescribed by roles and role expectations. Circumstances are evaluated by universal criteria as embodied in policies, rules, and protocols. Acceptance is conditional. The more a person cooperates with the organization and achieves for the organization, the more likely will she or he be accepted. Relationships are competitive. Not all concerns of members are legitimate. Legitimate concerns are bounded by roles rather than needs. Subjectivity is frowned upon. Rationality is prized. Self-interest prevails. These characteristics seem all too familiar in our schools.

The need for community becomes urgent when we consider the consequences of its loss. Students who are fortunate enough to experience belonging from family, extended family, friends, and neighbors feel attached and loved, experience the warmth and safety of intimacy, and are more cooperative and trusting of others. At an earlier time we took these values for granted. But today, in the words of Alamo Heights (Texas) superintendent Charles Slater, too often "we have lost vital parts of a good education: the neighborhood and family. While we cannot return to a simpler time, we must still find ways to give children a secure place to grow up, an opportunity to play and create and a chance to converse with adults" (1993, p. 6B).

In some respects the Native American and Native Canadian experience still hangs on to these values. As Brendtro, Brokenleg, and Van Bockern (1990) point out, "In traditional Native society, it was the duty of all adults to serve as teachers for younger persons. Child rearing was not just the province of biological parents but children were nurtured within a larger circle of significant others. From the earliest days of life, the child experienced a network of caring adults" (p. 37). And further, kinship "was not strictly a matter of biological relationships, but rather a learned way of viewing those who share a community of residence. The ultimate test of kinship was behavior, not blood: You belonged if you acted like you belonged" (p. 37). Citing the work of Karl Menninger, Brendtro, Brokenleg, and Van Bockern observe that "today's children are desperately pursuing 'artificial belongings' because this need is not being fulfilled by families, schools, and neighborhoods" (p. 38).

When students experience a loss of community they have two options: to create substitutes for this loss, and to live without community, with negative psychological consequences. Unfortunately, the substitutes that young people create are often dysfunctional or distorted. Using belonging as the value, Brendtro, Brokenleg, and Van Bockern summarize some of the consequences of this loss:

Belonging

Normal	*Distorted*	*Absent*
Attached	Gang loyalty	Unattached
Loving	Craves affection	Guarded
Friendly	Craves acceptance	Rejected
Intimate	Promiscuous	Lonely
Gregarious	Clinging	Aloof
Cooperative	Cult vulnerable	Isolated
Trusting	Overly dependent	Distrustful

Some youth who feel rejected are struggling to find artificial, distorted belongings through behavior such as attention seeking or running with gangs. Others have abandoned the pursuit and are reluctant to form human attachments. In either case, their unmet needs can be addressed by corrective relationships of trust and intimacy [p. 47].

A recent report from the National Commission on Children highlights the problems America faces with loss of community. West Virginia senator John D. Rockefeller, who chaired the commission, reported that "most American families are making heroic efforts" to maintain strong and close family ties. He noted also that "too little time, too little money, too many absent parents and overwhelming fears about children's health and safety are tearing at the seams of family life" (Cohen, 1991, p. 4). Eighty-eight percent of Americans who responded to the commission survey said it was harder to be a parent today than it used to be, 81 percent said that parents did not spend enough time with their children, 76 percent said that parents often did not know where their children were. More than half of the respondents said children are worse off today than they were ten years ago with respect to moral and religious training and parental supervision and discipline. Fully a third said that children get less love and care from parents than they did a decade ago.

Families fail for many reasons and often despite parents' heroic efforts. When families fail, children sometimes withdraw inward, hardening their shells and insulating themselves from the outside. But the typical response is for them to create their own "families" by turning to each other for support. Gangs, for example, provide the security, affection, and sense of belonging missing from other sources. Norms are important to young people, particularly to adolescents. In schools powerful and extensive norms systems develop that constitute a student subculture. Like any other culture these norms dictate not only how students should dress, the latest "in" language, and other harmless rituals of school life but also how students should think, what they are to value and believe, and how they should behave.

Participating in an identifiable student subculture is a healthy part of the transformation from adolescence to adulthood. But as the student subculture continues to distance itself from the mainstream norms of school and society, it strengthens its hold on what students think, believe, and do, not only about the relatively innocent rituals of adolescent life but about their studies, gang membership, sex, and alcohol and other drug abuse. A growing student subculture of this kind can come to dominate the legitimate culture of the school. When this happens, parents, teachers and principals lose control.

It is one thing to acknowledge loss of community. But

proposing that schools provide substitutes for this loss can cause problems. Do we really want the school to replace the family and neighborhood? The answer of course is no. At the national level we need to commit ourselves in both rhetoric and policy to putting families and neighborhoods first. In the meantime, community building in schools can provide an important safety net as an interim strategy. Further, as schools become communities, they facilitate the strengthening of family and neighborhood.

Tönnies's use of *gemeinschaft* and *gesellschaft* as polar opposites along a continuum is an example of a strategy in sociology with a long tradition. *Gemeinschaft* and *gesellschaft* represent ideal types that do not exist in the real world in pure forms. They are, instead, mental representations that can help us categorize and explain the opposites, on the one hand, and track movement along this continuum on the other (Weber, 1949, p. 90).

Thus schools are never *gemeinschaft* or *gesellschaft*. They possess characteristics of both. Even though I argue that the balance of emphases is seriously out of kilter in most schools, it is important to recognize that the *gesellschaft* perspective is both valuable and inescapable. We live, after all, in a *gesellschaft* world—a society characterized by technical rationality. And technical rationality has brought us many gains. Without *gesellschaft* we would not have a successful space program or heart transplant technology. Nor would we have great universities, profitable corporations, and workable governmental systems. There would be no hope of cleaning up the environment and we would not be able to defend ourselves. But *gesellschaft* brings with it its own kind of problems. As *gesellschaft* strengthens, *gemeinschaft* weakens. As *gemeinschaft* weakens, we experience a loss of community with all of its negative consequences.

In the extreme both *gemeinschaft* and *gesellschaft* create problems. As management expert Peter Drucker explains, "Unlike 'community,' 'society,' or 'family,' organizations are purposely designed and always specialized. Community and society are defined by the bonds that hold their members together . . . an organization is defined by its task" (1992, p. 100). He states further, "Society, community and family are all conserving institutions. They try to maintain stability and to prevent, or at least to slow, change. But the modern organization is a destabilizer. . . it must be organized for the systematic abandonment of whatever is established, customary, familiar, and comfortable. . . . In short, it must be organized for constant change" (p. 96).

Too much *gemeinschaft*, in other words, blocks progress. By the same token, too much *gesellschaft* creates loss of community. The answer is not to turn the clock back to a more romantic *gemeinschaft* world, but *to build gemeinschaft within gesellschaft*. We need to decide which theory should dominate which spheres of our lives. Most everyone will agree that the family, the extended family, and the neighborhood should be dominated by *gemeinschaft* values. The corporation, the research laboratory, and the court system, on the other hand, might well lean more toward *gesellschaft* values.

In modern times the school has been solidly ensconced in the *gesellschaft* camp (see for example Tyack and Hanson, 1982) with unhappy results. It is time that the school was moved from the *gesellschaft* side of the ledger to the *gemeinschaft* side. It is time that the metaphor for school was changed from formal organization to community.

2

Relationships
in Communities

Two hundred and forty students and nine teachers constitute a community within the Robert E. Lee High School in San Antonio, Texas. The students recruited to this "Challenger" program are considered "at risk," not for lack of intellectual ability but for reasons of poor academic performance. The Challenger strategy is to adopt middle school ways of thinking about teaching and learning within the high school and to provide learning experiences equal to those found in advanced placement and honors classes. This strategy emerged from an overall vision to create a living and learning community within the school. Beginning with its first class of eighty-two students recruited in 1990, the Challenger program now includes three classes.

At the end of the first year students were asked what they thought of their experiences. Here are examples of their comments (Molina, Fish, and Boyle, 1991).

> The thing I really like the most is the communication. Communication is important to all the Challengers and also trust.

> The teachers help us a lot by changing the way they teach.

> I thought everything about the program was great especially the teachers. I mean, they are always there when you need them and you can talk to them

if you have a problem, and they will listen, they won't ignore you.

Everyone learns to help others and trust one another.

The Challenger program has made me think positive about myself and the things I can do.

I think the teaching methods are good. They make people feel good about themselves and if you have a problem they try to help you.

What made this class different from others was that I actually got to think instead of just writing things down. I also learned people knowledge, not just book knowledge. P.S. Thanks for helping me get my mind off all the trouble I get into!!!

I like the teachers' open words and truthful actions.

To tell you the truth the thing I liked best about this class was you never really got mad or pissed off for things like some teachers would have in the same situation. Thanks.

The teachers actually want the students' opinions.

To tell you honestly I was never good in school and my grades sux. So more or less you're doing a great job.

I feel a lot smarter than I did last year. I was very lucky to be chosen for this program because I wouldn't have made it without the program.

We all became a family.

Algebra was really difficult but I studied and worked. Those are the best grades I have ever made in my whole life.

When I was in elementary and middle school no
one liked me so I didn't do well. Now people like me
and I'm doing better.

If it had not been for this program, I would have left
school after my 8th grade year. My dad did that. I
have watched him struggle. I'm not going to do that.
I want a higher education.

My home life is not safe. I never feel safe there. I do
feel safe when I am at school. . . with my teachers. . . with the other Challengers [pp. 18–19].

In commenting on his experiences, Challenger teacher
John Douglas notes, "Moving from a traditional classroom to the
Challenger Program has had startling effects on the students
and me. I am able to be a gestalt teacher, putting emphasis not
only on curriculum, but also developing a bond with the students that goes far beyond the student-teacher relationship I
have experienced in the past. I am their friend, advisor, confi-
dant, therapist, conscience, role model—in short, I am their
parent. I have provided them with a refuge from home lives
which are often dangerous and seemingly always in disarray.
The benefits of this relationship for the students are very similar
to the benefits for me. I feel loved, needed, and a sense of
community; the students do also" (p. 20). Teacher Drucie Mac-
Rae adds, "The reason I took this job was I was ready for a new
professional challenge. This year has been a voyage of professional self-discovery. These students have grown but so have I. We
are a family" (p. 20).

As part of the second-year evaluation of the program,
Challenger students were compared with a matched group of
non-Challenger students regarding their propensity to drop out
(Berg, 1992). When asked, "What are the chances of dropping
out?" Challenger students responded, "Slim chance," citing close
relationships with teachers, a climate of caring, and familylike
ties as the reasons. In the words of one Challenger student, "I like
being in this group. It's like a family. You feel so lucky sometimes
that you belong to a group." Non-Challenger students, by con-

trast, portrayed a fatalistic feeling of hopelessness. As one said, "If I keep failing as much as I am now, I probably will [drop out]. Why should I be here? I'm just wasting my time because I am failing" (p. 19).

Values, beliefs, norms, and other dimensions of community may be more important than the relationships themselves. But it is the web of relationships that stands out and it is through the quality and character of relationships that values, beliefs, and norms are felt.

A recent report issued by the Institute for Education and Transformation at the Claremont Graduate School (1992) points to quality of relationships and other relationship themes as the critical leverage point for school improvement. As the relationships go, so goes the school. Or, in the words of Claremont president John Maguire, "If the relationships are wrong between teachers and students, for whatever reason, you can restructure until the cows come home, but transformation won't take place" (Rothman, 1992, p. 1).

The Claremont researchers spent eighteen months studying four culturally diverse schools — two elementary, a middle, and a high school. They interviewed students, teachers, custodians, secretaries, cafeteria workers, parents, and others inside the schools. Over 24,000 pages of data were collected and analyzed. "Our data strongly suggests that the heretofore identified *problems* of schooling (lowered achievement, higher dropout rates and problems in the teaching profession) are rather *consequences* of much deeper and more fundamental problems" (Institute for Education and Transformation, 1992, p. 11).

These deeper, more fundamental problems pointed to seven major issues that surfaced repeatedly throughout the study and are summarized here. Relationship themes are embedded in each of these issues, with relationships itself the most important.

1. *Relationships.* Participants feel the crisis inside schools is directly linked to human relationships. Most often mentioned were relationships between teachers and students. Where positive things about the schools were noted, they usually in-

volve reports of individuals who care, listen, understand, respect others and are honest, open and sensitive. Teachers report their best experiences in school are those where they connect with students and are able to help them in some way. They also report, however, there is precious little time during the day to seek out individual students. . . . Students of color, especially older students often report that their teachers, school staff and other students neither like nor understand them. Many teachers also report they do not always understand students ethnically different than themselves. When relationships in schools are poor, fear, name calling, threats of or incidents of violence, as well as a sense of depression and hopelessness exist. This theme was prominently stated by participants and so deeply connected to all other themes in the data that it is believed this may be one of the two most central issues in solving the crisis inside schools.

2. *Race, culture, and class.* A theme which ran through every other issue, like that of relationships, was that of race, culture and class. This is a theme with much debate and very little consensus. Many students of color and some Euro-American students perceive schools to be racist and prejudiced, from the staff to the curriculum. Some students doubt the very substance of what is being taught. . . . Teachers are tremendously divided on such issues. Some are convinced that students are right about racism, others are not. . . . Students have an intense interest in knowing about one another's culture but receive very little of that knowledge from home or school.

3. *Values.* There are frequently related conversations in the United States that suggest people of color and/or people living in economically depressed areas hold different basic values than others, and that it is these differences which create conflicts in schools and society. While cultural differences clearly do exist in the expression or prioritization of values, our data hold no evidence that people inside schools have significantly different fundamental values. Our data suggest that parents, teachers, students, staff and administrators of all ethnicities and classes, value and desire education, honesty, integrity, beauty, care, jus-

tice, truth, courage and meaningful hard work. Participants' writings and transcripts of discussions are filled with references to basic values. However, very little time is spent in classrooms discussing these issues and a number of restrictions exist against doing so. In the beginning of our research many participants initially assumed other participants held different values. The more we talked, the more this assumption was challenged. Students desire a network of adults (parents and teachers) with whom they can "really talk about important things," and want to have these conversations about values with one another.

4. *Teaching and learning.* Students, especially those past fifth grade, frequently report that they are bored in school and see little relevance of what is taught to their lives and their futures. Teachers feel pressure to teach what is mandated and sometimes doubt its appropriateness for their students. Teachers also are often bored by the curriculum they feel they must teach. . . . Students from all groups, remedial and advanced, high school to elementary, desire both rigor and fun in their schoolwork. They express enthusiasm about learning experiences that are complex but understandable, full of rich meanings and discussions of values, require their own action, and those about which they feel they have some choice.

5. *Safety.* Related to disconnected relationships and not knowing about one another's differences is the issue of safety. Very few participants on campus or parents feel schools are safe places. This is particularly true in our middle school and high school. Teachers, students and staff fear physical violence. The influence of drugs, gangs and random violence is felt by students. Students feel physically safest inside classrooms and least safe in large gatherings between classes or traveling to or from school.

6. *Physical environment.* Students want schools that reflect order, beauty, space and contain rich materials and media. The desire for clean, aesthetically pleasing and physically comfortable spaces is expressed by all. The food served to students is a persistent complaint. Many would like foods more typical of

their homes and home cultures. The lack of any significant personal space such as lockers is problematic to students and also leads to feelings of being devalued. The depressed physical environment of many schools, especially those in lower socioeconomic areas, is believed by participants to reflect society's lack of priority for these children and their education.

7. *Despair, hope and the process of change.* Many participants feel a hopelessness about schools that is reflected in the larger society and in the music and art of our youth. Paradoxically, hope seemed to emerge following honest dialogues about our collective despair. Participants are anxious for change and willing to participate in change they perceive as relevant. We have strong indications that change inside schools might best be stimulated through participatory processes. In these self-driven research processes, participants came to openly discuss their hopes and dreams. Through this process, we understood there were shared common values around which we could begin to imagine a more ideal school (Institute for Education and Transformation, 1992, pp. 12–16).

The problematic relationships described in the report are the kinds of relationships that seem inevitably to evolve whenever schools are viewed as formal organizations. Further, it's not likely that relationships will improve unless this view is abandoned in favor of community.

Defining Relationship Patterns

How are relationships within communities different from those in formal organizations? The sociologist Talcott Parsons (1951, pp. 58–66) used Tönnies's concepts to describe different types of social relations. He argued that any social relationship can be described as a pattern made up of five pairs of variables that represent choices between alternative value orientations. A party to any relationship, for example, has to make decisions as to how she or he orients self to the other party. These decisions reflect the larger culture that circumscribes the relationship. As a group, the decisions represent a pattern of relationships, giving rise to Parsons's term "pattern variables." The pairs of variables that compose this pattern are listed below:

affective — affective neutrality
collective orientation — self-orientation
particularism — universalism
ascription — achievement
diffuseness — specificity

In schools, principals, teachers, and students have to make decisions about how they will perform their respective roles in relationship to others. Teachers, for example, have to decide: Will relationships with students be more that of a professional expert who treats students as if they were clients (affective neutrality)? Or, will relationships be more that of a parent, with students treated as if they were family members (affective)? Will students be given equal treatment in accordance with uniform standards, rules, and regulations (universalism)? Or, will students be treated more preferentially and individually (particularism)? Will role relationships and job descriptions narrowly define specific topics for attention and discussion with students (specificity)? Or, will relationships be considered unbounded by roles and thus more inclusive and holistic (diffuseness)? Will students have to earn the right to be regarded as "good" and to maintain their standing in the school (achievement)? Or, will students be accepted completely, simply because they have enrolled in the school (ascription)? Do we decide that a certain distance needs to be maintained in order for professional interests and concerns to remain uncompromised (self-orientation)? Or, do we view ourselves as part of a student-teacher "we" that compels us to work closely with students in identifying common interests, concerns, and standards for decision making (collective orientation)?

Parsons believed that the five pairs of pattern variables, when viewed as polar opposites on a continuum, can be used to evaluate the extent to which social relationships in an enterprise resemble *gemeinschaft* and *gesellschaft*. For example, though no school can be described as emphasizing affective relationships all the time or never emphasizing affective relationships, schools can be fixed on this continuum based on the relative emphasis given to each of the polar opposites. This fixing across several pairs of variables can provide us with a kind of cultural DNA (a pattern of variables, in Parsons's language) that can be used to place the school on the *gemeinschaft–gesellschaft* continuum.

To illustrate the five pairs of variables (and two other pairs that are closely related) I ask you to participate in a thought exercise. In the test below, the continuum is represented in the form of a schedule, and the two extreme ends of the spectrum are described. Think of a school that you know well, and consider three kinds of relationships in that school: the way teachers relate to students, the way teachers relate to each other, and the way administrators relate to teachers. In each case place a mark on the line scale in the schedule that best places the relationship.

Affective Versus Affective Neutrality

The parties that make up the relationship are always interested in each other—or, at the other extreme, are always disinterested. Actions toward each other are always determined by emotions (feelings of kinship, duty, or love)—or are always devoid of feelings. In the first instance teachers always relate to students as if they were teaching their own children. In the second instance teachers always relate to students as skilled technicians who apply objective treatments to students who are clients. Principals are emotionally involved as they work with and relate to teachers—or they adopt an emotionally detached, neutral attitude.

	Affective										*Affective neutrality*
Teacher-student	5	4	3	2	1	0	1	2	3	4	5
Among teachers	5	4	3	2	1	0	1	2	3	4	5
Administrator-teachers	5	4	3	2	1	0	1	2	3	4	5

Collective Orientation Versus Self-Orientation

The parties that make up the relationship are always motivated by common interests—or are always motivated by self-interest. In the first instance any particular action or situation is always evaluated in terms of its collective significance as defined by agreed-upon values that constitute a public moral code. In the second instance any particular action or situation is always evaluated in terms of personal significance by a private standard. At one extreme teachers, for example, always choose to help each other get ready for teacher evaluations or to plan for the new year, as a reflection of their commitment to a shared sense of success. Or, at the other extreme, teachers always choose to face teacher evaluations or to plan for the new year individually and privately as they compete with each other in pursuit of more personal gains. Principals are concerned with being sure that the best decisions are made even if lines of authority have to be compromised, or they are concerned with maintaining proper lines of authority and thus insist on making decisions.

	Collective orientation								Self- orientation	
Teacher-student	5	4	3	2	1	0	1	2	3	4	5
Among teachers	5	4	3	2	1	0	1	2	3	4	5
Administrator-teachers	5	4	3	2	1	0	1	2	3	4	5

Particularism Versus Universalism

The parties that make up the relationship always size up situations and make decisions on the basis of specifics that define that situation—or always on the basis of general protocols and rules. Actions are governed entirely by the particulars of the relationship itself—or actions are governed entirely by the universal norms of the system itself. In the first instance teachers always take into consideration the unique circumstances that define a discipline problem and then always create a unique resolution based on this consideration. Thus, the same discipline problem may be handled differently on different occasions. In the second instance discipline problems are always categorized by predetermined protocols and then always dealt with according to universal rules. Thus, the same discipline problem is always handled the same way whenever it appears. Teachers judge students in accordance with particular and specific standards, and the standards vary with students — or teachers judge students by universal standards, and the standards do not vary with the students.

	Particularism										*Universalism*
Teacher-student	5	4	3	2	1	0	1	2	3	4	5
Among teachers	5	4	3	2	1	0	1	2	3	4	5
Administrator-teachers	5	4	3	2	1	0	1	2	3	4	5

Ascription Versus Achievement

The parties that make up the relationship always value each other for who and what they are regardless of their achievements — or always value each other for what they accomplish. Each always accepts the other as an absolute — or acceptance is always contingent on one's achievements. In the first instance students are always accepted, considered "good," and loved regardless of how well they do in school and how much they achieve. In the second instance acceptance, attributions of being a good person, and love are always contingent upon and distributed based on the extent to which students are cooperative and achieve. Teachers accept each other, help each other, and respect each other because they are members of the same school faculty — or they accept, help, and respect each other differentially, in accordance with perceptions of relative worth and relative achievement.

	Ascription									Achievement
Teacher-student	5	4	3	2	1	0	1	2	3	4	5
Among teachers	5	4	3	2	1	0	1	2	3	4	5
Administrator-teachers	5	4	3	2	1	0	1	2	3	4	5

Diffuseness Versus Specificity

The parties that make up the relationship always view each other in less defined ways that allow for broad interaction and for concern that is widely defined — or always view each other in ways defined more narrowly by roles, role expectations, and preset work requirements. In the first instance everything about the person is always relevant on any given occasion. In the second instance relevance is always determined by role requirements and the requirements of the task at hand. Principals always view teachers as whole persons to be engaged fully — or always as cases to be treated in accordance with proper role definitions and expectations. Teachers are bonded to each other as total personalities who constitute a "family" — or relate to each other in more limited ways as defined by their jobs.

	Diffuseness									Specificity
Teacher-student	5	4	3	2	1	0	1	2	3	4	5
Among teachers	5	4	3	2	1	0	1	2	3	4	5
Administrator-teachers	5	4	3	2	1	0	1	2	3	4	5

One important characteristic that differentiates *gemeinschaft* from *gesellschaft* is the relationship between means and ends. In *gesellschaft* a clear distinction is made between the two, a distinction that communicates an instrumental view of human nature and society. Within *gemeinschaft*, by contrast, the distinctions are blurred. Ends remain ends but means too are considered as ends.

On the corporate farm, for example, the land is viewed instrumentally as a means to raise crops for sale with the end being profits. Profits are important as well to the traditional family farm, but the land is not likely to be viewed quite so instrumentally. It is, instead, considered to be sacred in its own right, something to be treasured—a legacy to be passed down to subsequent generations. The land, in this case, becomes an important tie that bonds people who identify with it together into a "we" and provides them with meaning and significance. This distinction between means as ends (substantive) and means to ends (instrumental) adds a sixth pair to the schedule that can be used to evaluate your school.

In schools that resemble communities, for example, teachers care about the subjects they teach. They communicate to students that what is being taught is valuable in its own right and not a mere means to some end. Reverence for what is being taught is modeled by a spirit of inquiry and by the teacher's commitment to being a learner. This stance pays dividends in increased student learning. Many of the other pattern variables speak to the principle: "You need to know students well to teach them well." This one adds the principle: "You need to be passionate about what you teach if students are to value what is taught."

Substantive Versus Instrumental

The partners that make up the relationship always view means as ends equal to ends—or always make a clear distinction between means and ends. Discipline policies and rules are always considered to be moral standards to be celebrated in their own right—or are always considered as means to manage the behavior of students. The subjects taught are viewed entirely as knowledge to be valued and enjoyed—or are always viewed as content to be mastered in order to get good grades and high test scores. In the first instance principals emphasize improving the quality of the teachers' workplace because that is a good thing to do. In the second instance principals work to improve the quality of the teachers' workplace as a way to motivate them to perform. In the first instance students are fed because loving, compassionate people feed hungry children. In the second instance the purpose of the school breakfast program is to relieve the hunger

that keeps children from learning (Noddings, 1992, p. 13). Students study only because they value knowledge as an end in
itself—or only to win approval, get promoted, or perhaps to
qualify for the driver's education program.

	Substantive									Instrumental
Teacher-student	5	4	3	2	1	0	1	2	3	4	5
Among teachers	5	4	3	2	1	0	1	2	3	4	5
Administrator-teachers	5	4	3	2	1	0	1	2	3	4	5

Altruism Versus Egocentrism

Gemeinschaft and *gesellschaft* provide different ties for connecting
people to each other and for connecting them to their work. In
the school as community, relationships are both close and informal. Individual circumstances count. Acceptance is unconditional. Relationships are cooperative. Concerns of members are
unbounded, and thus considered legitimate as long as they
reflect needs. Subjectivity is okay. Emotions are legitimate. Sac-
rificing one's self-interest for the sake of other community members is common. Members associate with each other because
doing so is valuable as an end in itself. Knowledge is valued and
learned for its own sake, not just as a means to get something or
get somewhere. Children are accepted and loved because that's
the way one treats community members. These community
characteristics emerge in part because of the ties of kinship and
in part because of the sense of identity that is created by sharing
a common place such as a classroom or a school. But the ties that
bond and bind the most are those that emerge from a compact
of mutual shared obligations and commitments, a common
purpose. These are the ingredients needed to create a community of the mind.

Philosopher Mary Rousseau (1991) believes that the key to
determining whether community will be authentic or counterfeit is the motives that bring people together. To her it is altruistic love that differentiates authentic from counterfeit.

Words like "altruism" and "love" can make us uncomfortable. Our *gesellschaft* theories of schooling, I fear, have conditioned us to adopt an impersonal, bureaucratic, professional, managerial, and technical language. Students are clients to be treated and have problems to be solved. Learning is equated with training. Teaching becomes instruction. Deciding, sharing, and reflecting together is labeled "site-based management." Concerns about what we are doing, why we are doing it, and how well we are doing it become "total quality management." Students who are not interested in what is being taught and are showing it are "off task." I fear that this language distances us from the real concerns of people and the real problems of schooling. If we are going to be serious about community building, we are going to have to cross this language barrier by speaking more directly and more humanly about schooling.

To be blunt about it, we cannot achieve community unless we commit ourselves to the principle "love thy neighbor as thyself." Yes, these are sacred words but then again community is a sacred idea. Loving in this sense does not mean that I want to spend my summer vacation with my neighbor or that I want to become her or his telephone companion. It certainly does not mean falling in love in the romantic sense, or having other unusual feelings of affection, warmth, tenderness, or lust. These examples are more descriptive of egocentric love than altruistic love.

Egocentric love is emotionally and physically self-gratifying. When egocentric love is the motive, each of the parties to the relationship enter into an implicit contract with the other for the exchange of needs and satisfactions that benefit both. As Mary Rousseau points out, "Contracts, inherently egocentric in their motivation, can only link people in their external aspects. Contracts can bring people together in the same place at the same time, to share a common activity or project. But since those who love contractually are seeking their own fulfillment as their end, looking to other people as the means to their own pleasure or utility, they forge no existential bonds with each other" (p. 49).

Webster defines altruism as benevolent concern for the

welfare of others, as selflessness. Love is defined as deep devotion and good will that comes from and contributes to feelings
of brotherhood and sisterhood. Altruistic love is an expression
of selfless concern for others that stems from devotion or obligation. At its heart, altruistic love is more cultural than psychological. It can exist even if community by blood and community of
place are absent. Community of the mind is enough to sustain
altruistic love.

For example, teachers and administrators who work at
the central office are not physically close to teachers, administrators, and students in a particular school. Yet they can demonstrate altruistic love when motivated by devotion and duty and
when they show selfless concern for the welfare of that school.
When they do this, they qualify as members of that particular
community.

Strictly speaking, altruistic love and egocentric love are
not opposite poles of the same continuum. But arranging them
in this way is still useful for our purposes. Considering altruistic
and egocentric love provides us with another set of ideas that
can be used to evaluate the *gemeinschaft* and *gesellschaft* qualities
of a particular school.

	Altruistic love									Egocentric love
Teacher-student	5	4	3	2	1	0	1	2	3	4	5
Among teachers	5	4	3	2	1	0	1	2	3	4	5
Administrator-teachers	5	4	3	2	1	0	1	2	3	4	5

In sum, we can assess the extent to which relationships
within a school embody community by describing them using
Parsons's five pairs of pattern variables and two additional pairs
that constitute an extended pattern of seven. In Table 2.1, this
extended pattern is arranged in the form of an inventory, "Profile of Community." The more *gemeinschaft*-like is the pattern, the
more communitylike is the school. The more *gesellschaft*-like is
the pattern, the more appropriate is the metaphor "formal

Table 2.1. Profiles of Community.

School as Community (Gemeinschaft)		*School as Formal* *Organization* (Gesellschaft)
	Teacher's relationship with students *5 4 3 2 1 0 1 2 3 4 5*	
Affective	• • • • • • • • • • •	Affective neutrality
Collective orientation	• • • • • • • • • • •	Self-orientation
Particularism	• • • • • • • • • • •	Universalism
Ascription	• • • • • • • • • • •	Achievement
Diffuseness	• • • • • • • • • • •	Specificity
Substantive	• • • • • • • • • • •	Instrumental
Altruistic love	• • • • • • • • • • •	Ego-centered love
	Relationships among teachers *5 4 3 2 1 0 1 2 3 4 5*	
Affective	• • • • • • • • • • •	Affective neutrality
Collective orientation	• • • • • • • • • • •	Self-orientation
Particularism	• • • • • • • • • • •	Universalism
Ascription	• • • • • • • • • • •	Achievement
Diffuseness	• • • • • • • • • • •	Specificity
Substantive	• • • • • • • • • • •	Instrumental
Altruistic love	• • • • • • • • • • •	Ego-centered love
	Administrators' relationships with teachers *5 4 3 2 1 0 1 2 3 4 5*	
Affective	• • • • • • • • • • •	Affective neutrality
Collective orientation	• • • • • • • • • • •	Self-orientation
Particularism	• • • • • • • • • • •	Universalism
Ascription	• • • • • • • • • • •	Achievement
Diffuseness	• • • • • • • • • • •	Specificity
Substantive	• • • • • • • • • • •	Instrumental
Altruistic love	• • • • • • • • • • •	Ego-centered love

organization." To extend our thought exercise, use the inventory to evaluate the relationships in Central Park East Secondary School, described in Chapter Three. Now use the same inventory to summarize the ratings of the relationships in the school you evaluated in this chapter. How do they compare? Try repeating this exercise for the Jackson-Keller School when you get to Chapter Ten.

Building community requires the development of a com-

munity of mind represented in shared values, conceptions, and
ideas about schooling and human nature. This mind structure
provides the community and its members with purpose and
meanings that are embodied in duties and obligations. Fulfilling these duties and obligations requires selfless behavior, altruistic love.

Not many schools can meet this exacting standard completely. Indeed it is probably the case that authentic community
can never be achieved in schools in pure form. But this reality
should not deter us from struggling to build community from
where we are now. What is important is that our quest for
community be a sincere one. The test of our sincerity is our
willingness to change the underlying theory of school itself.
Thomas Cardellichio, principal of the Bell School in Chappaqua, New York, makes the point this way, "As we think about
creating new visions of schools we must recognize that our
present structure impedes our vision. . . . We may create philosophies and standards and goals and missions, but the accom-
plishment of these visions will be restrained by the structures in
which they are achieved" (1992, p. 3).

The Waterloo Region Catholic School Board in Ontario
has made a commitment to create schools as inclusive communities. Their vision is powerful and their stance is realistic.
Community building, as they understand it, is a struggle to find
purpose. According to Waterloo administrators George Flynn
and Maureen Innes: "Community does not develop naturally. It
requires tremendous struggle, and the answers to all the tough
questions are in the struggle. The struggle, though, is essential
because the children we teach will not care how much we know
until they know how much we care" (1992, p. 203). The relationships that define our roles as teachers to students, among
teachers, and as administrators to teachers communicate how
much we care. If we desire community in schools, we have no
choice but to make them increasingly *gemeinschaft*. Flynn and
Innes explain, "It seems that a school that is a true community is
a group of individuals who have learned to communicate hon-

estly with one another; who have built relationships that go deeper than their composures; and who have developed some significant commitment to rejoice together, mourn together, delight in each other, and make others' conditions their own" (p. 203).

3

Emerging
School Communities

Many schools are now deeply involved in community building. The Central Park East Secondary School in East Harlem, New York, and the Köln-Holweide Comprehensive School in Cologne, Germany, are celebrated examples. Both are frequently cited in the media and in the literature. In this chapter I provide examples of community by kinship, community of place, and community of mind by describing community building at CPESS and at the Köln-Holweide school. These models illustrate as well a clear tilt toward relationships characterized as *gemeinschaft* in Chapter Two. And they lay the groundwork for discussions of other facets of community building that appear in subsequent chapters. Two other examples of community building, less celebrated but equally worthy, are discussed in Chapters Nine and Ten: the Denali School in Fairbanks, Alaska, and the Jackson-Keller School in San Antonio. Denali School is used to illustrate what it means to become a community of learners and the Jackson-Keller School what it means to become a community of leaders.

Describing models of community can be intimidating. Some readers will think, "These schools have reinvented them-

Note: For descriptions of CPESS I rely on conversations with Herb Rosenfeld (1992) and on articles written by Deborah Meier as sources. Rosenfeld and Meier were cofounders of the school, with Meier serving as its director and Rosenfeld as assistant director and as a math teacher. For descriptions of Köln-Holweide, I rely on an interview with the school principal, Anne Ratzki, published in *American Educator* ("Creating a School Community...," 1988).

selves. They have changed everything. I like what I am reading but what can I do? I am only a teacher. I am only a principal. I don't control things around here!" Yes, these schools have reinvented themselves. They are places where community runs deep. You can sense that in the ways in which people relate to each other, in the curriculum that has been created, in the ways teaching and learning are done. By contrast, community probably doesn't run quite so deep in your school. At least not right now. But it can. And you don't have to start big.

Community can begin with you and your state of mind. A single teacher, for example, in a single classroom within the most *gesellschaft* of schools can decide to make that classroom a place where community flourishes. One classroom can turn into two, and then four. A single principal can model community in voice, temperament, and behavior.

From such modest beginnings community will take hold, then strengthen and eventually deepen. I make this assertion because community is part of our human nature (a theme elaborated on in Chapter Four). Community may be lost in some places and pushed to the side in other places but once it is revived, people respond. We want the ties that community offers, ties that bond us to others and bind us to ideas that give meaning to our lives. The schools described here and in Chapters Nine and Ten are successful in building community because enough people decided to become on the outside what deep inside they already were.

Central Park East Secondary School (CPESS) was founded as a public secondary school in East Harlem, New York, in the fall of 1985. Beginning with eighty seventh-graders, the school has grown by one grade each year since, becoming 7–12 in the fall of 1990. The school is located in District 4 of the New York City Public School System, an administrative unit known for its commitment to decentralization and small schools. District 4 is composed of fifty-two different schools but only twenty school buildings. In District 4, schools are collections of people rather than spaces bounded by brick and mortar.

CPESS is a school of about 450 students (90 percent minority with 60 percent eligible for free lunch) that shares a

building with two other schools. One of the values that constitutes CPESS's community of mind is a commitment to personalized schooling. Believing that to teach a child well, one must
know that child well, the people of CPESS set 450 students as an
informal cap. They believe it would be better to spin off a CPESS
II than to grow much beyond 450.

For Deborah Meier, the founding director of the school,
the metaphor for creating CPESS was the kindergarten. To her
the kindergarten tradition of teaching, learning, and schooling
made enough sense for it to be the frame for thinking about
schooling at all levels. In her words:

> Kindergarten was the one place—maybe the last
> place—where you were expected to know children
> well, even if they didn't hand in their homework,
> finish their Friday tests, or pay attention. Kinder-
> garten teachers know that learning must be person-
> alized, just because kids are idiosyncratic. . . . Kin-
> dergarten teachers know that helping children
> learn to become more self-reliant is part of their
> task—starting with tying shoes and going to the
> bathroom. Catering to children's growing indepen-
> dence is a natural part of a kindergarten child's
> classroom life. It is, alas, the last time children are
> given independence, encouraged to make choices,
> and allowed to move about on their own steam. The
> older they get the less we take into account the
> importance of their own interests. In kindergarten
> we design our rooms for real work—not just passive
> listening. We put things in the room that will ap-
> peal to children, grab their interests, and engage
> their minds and hearts. Teachers in kindergarten
> are editors, critics, cheerleaders, and caretakers,
> not just lecturers or deliverers of instruction [1991,
> p. 136].

Community of kinship is embodied in the kindergarten metaphor because kindergarten emphasizes personalized rela-

tionships and feelings of closeness in both learning and life. Since "kindergarten" communicates a theory of schooling, its acceptance contributes to the strengthening of a community of mind at CPESS.

Another value that contributes to this community of mind is the shared belief that students are "workers" and teachers are "coaches." This belief was informed by CPESS's charter membership in Ted Sizer's Coalition of Essential Schools. Student-as-worker connects with the belief that students learn best by doing and that the best learning takes place when ideas are embedded in a context of meaning. Realizing these beliefs led CPESS to emphasize interdisciplinary studies, problems-oriented teaching, and exhibitions of mastery as overarching frameworks for planning and evaluating student experiences.

Another aspect of CPESS's Essential Schools heritage is its commitment to doing a few things well rather than attempting to cover, albeit thinly and often abstractly, a more comprehensive curriculum. The curriculum, for example, is organized around two main academic themes—humanities and math-science. Humanities includes the study of literature, history, social studies, and fine arts as one single curriculum. Two hours are spent each day in one academic theme and two hours in the other.

In addition there is one hour each day for something called the advisory, in which between ten and fifteen students meet with a faculty member. All faculty members, including the director and support staff, are responsible for an advisory. The formal academic schedule is rounded off with one hour of foreign language (Spanish) each morning. Another hour is devoted to lunch, physical education, conferences, library use, and use of computers. From 3:00 to 5:00 P.M. the building is open for sports programs, doing homework, working on class projects, and participating in student-initiated clubs.

The CPESS schedule makes it possible to reduce maximum class size to twenty. Students work with only three different teachers each day. Both of these factors contribute to the development of strong personal relationships among teachers and between teachers and students.

Both community by kinship and community of mind contribute to and are in return strengthened by community of place — a close association with others that is bounded by space and sustained over time. The school, for example, is divided into three major divisions, each containing about 150 students. Students spend two years in each division. Division I corresponds to grades seven and eight, and Division II to grades nine and ten. Division III, called the Senior Institute, contains the "final" two years of study. Actually, students stay in the Senior Institute for as long as it takes for them to complete the necessary exhibitions of mastery to earn their diplomas. Within divisions, no distinctions are made by grade level and everyone takes the same courses. Each division is divided once again into two houses of about seventy-five students. Each house has its own faculty of four or five members. Though teachers bring special expertness from their respective disciplines to their teaching, they function as generalists by teaching in other areas as well. These grouping patterns make it possible for teachers to see about 40 students (as compared with the 150 or so in the traditional *gesellschaft* high school) each day.

The ties between what is taught, how it is taught, how one organizes for teaching and learning, and what one believes are strong at CPESS. Values such as personalized education, smallness, and treating students with deep respect are important. At the center, however, is not just a high regard for the psychological self but for the intellectual self as well. CPESS respects the minds of its students. This value is reflected in *The Promise*, CPESS's statement of purpose and mission (Central Park East Secondary School, 1988):

> At CPESS we make an important promise to every student — one we know we can keep. We promise our students that when they graduate from CPESS, they will have learned to use their minds — and to use their minds well.
>
> In every class, in every subject, students will learn to ask and to answer these questions:

1. From whose viewpoint are we seeing or reading or hearing? From what angle or perspective?
2. How do we know what we know? What is the
   evidence, and how reliable is it?
3. How are things, events or people connected to
   each other? What is the cause and what is the
   effect?
4. So what? Why does it matter? What does it all
   mean? Who cares?

We are committed to the idea that a diploma
is a meaningful piece of paper, not one that says
only that the student has "stuck it out" through high
school. A CPESS diploma tells the student—
and the world—that the student has not only mastered specific fields of study but is curious and
thoughtful, above all, has learned "how to learn"
and to use his/her learning to deal with new issues
and problems.

CPESS believes that families should be treated with respect. It is very important that families (whether blood relatives
of students or not) be involved deeply and meaningfully. On this
theme, Deborah Meier (1991) states, "Respect between children's
families, their community, and the school is an end in itself, as
well as an essential means to the education we had in mind.
Education isn't merely a question of good and frequent contact
between school and family. The gap between the social, ethnic
and class histories of the school's staff and the school's families is
often substantial. It's a gap we cannot bridge entirely. However, at
minimum parents need to know that we will not undermine
their authority, their values or their standards. They need to
believe that we're not frustrating the aspirations that they have
for their kids, nor blaming them for what goes wrong with their
kids" (p. 142).
Neither students nor parents will receive the respect they

deserve unless teachers are respected. Respect at CPESS involves appreciating the capacities and abilities of teachers to perform, to grow, to self-sacrifice, and to help each other. Teachers are expected, for example, to behave collegially, and to take charge of their own practice by becoming autonomous selves who are bonded together by common values and by the need to cooperate with each other in order for everyone to be successful.

But to create a sense of "we" you need to start with healthy "I's." Deborah Meier says, "We are creating a staff-run school with high standards — the staff must know each other well, be familiar with each other's work, and know how the school operates. Each team of teachers that works with the same students and the same curriculum teaches at the same time. The school's structure, from the placement of classes to the scheduling of the day, is organized to enable teachers to visit each other's rooms, to reflect on their own and their colleagues' practice, and to give each other full support" (1991, p. 144).

Not only do teachers teach in collaborative settings but this is also the way decisions are made. Meier (1992) explains:

> Decisions are made as close to each teacher's own classroom setting as possible, although all decisions are ultimately the responsibility of the whole staff. The decisions are not merely on minor matters — length of classes or the number of field trips. The teachers collectively decide on content, pedagogy, and assessment as well. They teach what they think matters. The "whole staff" is not enormous — none of our Central Park East schools is larger than about 450 students, most are 200 to 300. That means a faculty that can sit in a circle in one room and get a chance to hear each other. Governance is simple. There are virtually no permanent standing committees. Finally, we work together to develop assessment systems for our students, their families, ourselves, and the broader public — systems that represent our values and beliefs in as direct a manner as possible. When we are asked "Does it work?"

we have had a voice in deciding what "work" means
(p. 607).

The sense of "we" that characterizes the faculty is the same
kind of relationship that teachers seek with students. Marian
Mogalescu (Lockwood, 1990), a humanities teacher at CPESS,
states, "In the two-hour period [each day for each of the academic themes] we have time to work intimately with the kids,
help them plug in personally to the material, work step by step
because kids learn at different rates. It's the conversation and
students working with students as well as with the teacher over a
long period of time that really produces substantial movement"
(p. 9). She continues, "There are many, many times when I don't
know the answer, but it's the collaboration between staff and the
joint inquiry that makes what we're doing very powerful. When I
first came to this school, I wondered if I could be in control if I
wasn't standing in front of the room. What happened is that I'm
the manager, in a sense, but it's shared control. Together we—
students and teachers—control and direct the discussion and
the focus of the material" (p. 10).

The typical classroom resembles a real workplace. Every
student has a job to do. Students work in groups on intellectually
rigorous subject matter that is presented in the context of real-
life problems. The teacher acts as a mentor to each of the groups
and to each individual student. Not only do teachers provide
frameworks, assistance, and support but by being involved with
the students as learners themselves and as learning coaches, they
model higher-order thinking processes and problem-solving
skills. The community of mind that students and teachers share
has as its center the importance of providing students with
intellectually challenging rigorous academic experiences that
will make them resourceful lifelong learners.

The Köln-Holweide Comprehensive School in Cologne,
Germany, represents still another model of community in the
making. Köln-Holweide shares with CPESS a commitment to
personalized relationships among teachers and between teachers and students, to smallness, cooperation, collegiality, respect
for the student's personality, and respect for the student's mind.

The two schools also share some common ways to embody these values. But unlike CPESS's commitment to the Essential Schools platform (believing that "less is more" and using exhibitions of mastery as the organizing framework for planning and evaluating student learning experiences), Köln-Holweide's approach to curriculum, teaching, and evaluation seems a little more "traditional" in its comprehensiveness. Köln-Holweide is part of a network of twenty schools that share a commitment to the same approach to schooling.

Köln-Holweide seeks to become a community by kinship, of place, and of mind by providing an environment in which students find support, get direction, and feel safe. To achieve this goal teachers are divided into autonomous teams, each responsible for one group of students. This approach, called the "Team–Small-Group Plan," is designed to diminish the loss of community and impersonality associated with the typical large modern high school and to provide a design for teaching and learning where students of different abilities and backgrounds work together to reach their full potential. Students are assigned to small, heterogeneous "table groups" made up of five to six students. Students are members of the same table group for at least a year and often more, sometimes throughout the six years of schooling.

Eighteen to twenty table groups constitute a larger grouping of students for which a team of six full-time equivalent teachers is responsible. Since it is common practice in Germany for two teachers to share one position the team may have up to eight different teachers. This aggregate group of students and their teachers remain together from the fifth grade until the tenth grade. Time is set aside for each day for members of the teaching team to meet and plan together. Teams are responsible for deciding how students will be grouped, how the school day will be organized, and which teachers will teach which subjects.

In 1988, *American Educator* magazine presented an interview with Anne Ratzki, headmistress of Köln-Holweide. The interview was based on discussions with the executive council, president, and staff members of the American Federation of

Teachers and is excerpted here ("Creating a School Community...," 1988, pp. 10–43).

Q. First, tell us a little about your students. How many are there? What kinds of families do they come from? How do they compare demographically to students in other German schools?

A. We have two thousand students. They are quite average and representative. The school is in a suburb, and we have an area where people own their own homes, but we also draw from public housing where residents are too poor or unstable to live anywhere else.

Although I can't cite statistics, I think about 25 percent of our children come from families in which the parents are unemployed. Sometimes we find the children ill clothed and hungry. Because they can't afford the few marks that some school activities cost, we run special fundraising activities. Because of divorce, many children live with only one parent, and they often have very big problems. . . .

Q. To get a sense of your school, let's start very broadly. Can you tell me the five ways in which you and your twenty sister schools most differ from traditional American schools?

A. Yes. First, our teachers do not work as isolated individuals, each trying to deal alone with myriad problems that plague his students and the school. They are part of a team of six to eight teachers — six if the teachers are all full time, seven or eight if several teachers share one or two positions. Together this team is responsible for the teaching and education of three groups of twenty-seven to thirty students — what we call classes.

Second, and this is probably the most important, our teachers are responsible not merely for teaching their subjects but for the total education of their students, for making sure that their students succeed, personally and academically. This requires us to cast our net broadly and involve ourselves with many things: We eat with the students, counsel them on personal and academic issues, determine their class schedules, tailor their curricula, help to broaden their interests by offering special lunchtime activities, talk with their parents.

Third, the teacher teams and their students stay together for six years, from the time the students enter the school in fifth grade until they earn their leaving certificate at the end of grade ten. And the students stay with their class of about thirty all these years also. The team's composition might change a little over the six years, but the idea is for the teachers and students to get to know each other very, very well and for the teachers and parents to get to know each other as well.

Fourth, our teachers make all the instructional decisions, including how the curriculum will be taught, and all sorts of other decisions as well. They develop a varied schedule of lunchtime activities and the class schedule, determining who will teach what and when, whether certain classes are best taught in a single period or a longer block of time or if more time should be provided for students to pursue independent study. They instigate inservice training as needed on different topics, they train new teachers and mentor each other, they arrange for someone to cover the class of an absent teacher, they call in social workers when that seems necessary. . . . Each team is really running a school within a school and has a great deal of autonomy. But that entails a great deal of responsibility also.

Fifth, our students are not forced to compete against each other in a destructive way. In the traditional school, students are pitted against each other at the earliest ages. . . .

In contrast, we try to give support to our students. When they first enter the school, they are assigned to a table group of five or six students, integrated by sex, ability, and ethnic origin. Inside these groups, the children tutor and encourage each other. It's an extension of what you call cooperative learning groups. The difference is that our children stay in these same table groups for every subject and normally for at least a year.

Q. How long is "at least a year"?

A. It depends. In any group there will be problems — personality conflicts and so forth. But we try not to just alter groups for this reason. We work with the students to help them overcome their problems. But if the conflicts are too severe, or if the team teachers see that a particular group just isn't learning well together, they will do some minor reshuffling. This probably happens about once a year. In the older grades, students will usually initiate their own minor reshuffling—which must gain teacher approval—also about once a year.

Q.   What about personality conflicts between a student and one of his teachers? Six years is a long time to endure each other. What is really gained from this sustained contact?

A.   A great deal is gained: First, if we know that a child is our responsibility for six years—that we can't pass him on to someone else—we are forced to come to terms with even the most difficult characters. And if you have a child for six years, not one—especially if you're sharing responsibility for him with six or eight teammates—you stand a chance of winning him over. You're not already defeated at the starting line. Second, we gain educational time: We don't lose several weeks each September learning a new set of names, teaching the basic rules to a new set of students, and figuring out exactly what they learned the previous year; and we don't lose weeks at the end of the year packing students back up. Most importantly, teachers and students get to know each other—teachers get to know how each student learns, and students know which teachers they can go to for various kinds of help. The importance of this is incalculable.

If a personality conflict between a teacher and student is terribly severe, in very rare, extreme cases, a switch of teams could be considered. But in all of our experience, that has never happened. . . .

Q.   So you have really transformed the role of the teacher.

A.   Not really. The teacher's role remains the same: to teach. Only the teaching technique has changed.

We found that teaching to the whole class when the students were of such varied abilities didn't work. When you speak to the whole class, you reach a limited number of students. We bore some of the brilliant ones, and we don't reach some of the very slow ones. Children learn early on how to give the appearance of attentiveness, but we have no idea what's happening behind their faces. We assume the children are "on task." But only those who are listening and understanding really are.

Our children are always busy and working, so it's harder to lose them, and they're always "on task." If a student has a problem, he doesn't have to wait for the teacher, he can ask his table group for help. If the group can't help, then the teacher will — but the first responsibility to help lies with the group. . . .

Q. You said the teachers have a great deal of autonomy and authority and you outlined for us a whole series of their responsibilities. So that we can understand a little better both what the teachers are doing and how the school runs, explain, for example, how the curriculum is developed.

A.   Take the mathematics curriculum. Our state's ministry of education publishes a small book that states what students should learn in each grade. We take that book and the textbook that we have selected and meet as a grade-level curriculum conference, composed of one delegate from each of the three teams in that grade. We decide which elements of the prescribed curriculum and which sections of what books should be emphasized and in what order they should be taught. We'll select or develop materials for each class, often developing special materials for the weaker or quicker children. Or, perhaps we'll agree on a good film to bring in.

Q.   So these are materials that would be used at the tables?

A.   That's right. These are materials that will help students understand what's in the textbook or that will take them beyond the text — handouts, exercises, additional readings, perhaps. Maybe we would develop a simulation game, questions to provoke a table discussion, or instructions and materials for preparing a new group project. But, remember, the individual teacher isn't designing all these group tasks all by him or herself. Three teachers are preparing the materials for all the subject teachers in the grade.

Q.   What if I don't like the materials the curriculum conference has prepared? Have I lost the freedom to develop the kind of lesson I want to give? Doesn't this become a terrible straitjacket for a teacher?

A. Not really. You are always free to bring your ideas to the conference. But most teachers believe that materials developed by the group will be better than those prepared by a single teacher in isolation. But certainly if someone wants to go his own way, that's okay. Why not? It's never good to force people to do what they don't want to.

Q. When does it [the curriculum conference] meet?

A. Let me explain the structure of the week. Every Tuesday afternoon, children leave at 1:30, and the afternoon is devoted to a variety of teacher conferences. Several times a year, the whole staff will meet together to discuss issues affecting the whole school. Periodically, all the teachers in a grade will get together. And every other week, teachers from each team meet to discuss such issues as the progress of individual students, groups that aren't working well, and modifications in the class schedule. Or if a teacher will be absent, they'll decide who will cover her classes. We never hire substitutes. Since they don't know the students, they are rarely able to do more than keep order. (In alternate weeks, team members often meet at someone's home and conduct their meeting over a friendly dinner. This is generally not resented because most teachers believe the regular meetings are necessary.)

As for the curriculum conferences, they are essentially subcommittees of the all-grade subject conferences that meet every sixth Tuesday. In this subject conference, the three teachers from every grade who are delegates to, say, an English curriculum conference will meet and discuss curriculum matters that affect all grades — which dictionary to use, for example, or whether to change the textbook. This is also where subject matter research is discussed. A new study on a more promising way to teach a mathematical concept, for example, would be discussed in the mathematics conference. . . .

In addition to developing materials, the curriculum conference may compare how different classes and teams did on the last round of tests. If one did particularly well, or not so well, we'll want to ask why. Then perhaps someone will volunteer to draft the next test, which will then be circulated to all the other

English teachers for their comments and approval. So at different times, everyone prepares something and then gives it to everyone else. . . .

Q. What about discipline problems? You must have some students who are incorrigible. What do you do with them?

A.   We do have children like that. These problems exist mostly in the lower grades, before we've really been able to work with the groups and individuals. The team teachers observe them and perhaps they'll talk with the parents, or, if the table group is strong enough to help, they'll talk with them. We may give the students additional work. We may call a psychologist. But there is rarely a problem we can't handle, because no teacher has to handle it alone. You put together the abilities and experience of six or eight teachers, and you can solve most problems. It sounds Pollyannaish. But it's true.

Q. Your teachers are supposed to be more than instructors — they're teachers, tutors, counselors, group facilitators, social workers. . . . Do they resent it? Do they wish it would all go away so they could focus on teaching their discipline?

A.   That's a good question. It's fiercely discussed here. In other German schools, especially in the *Gymnasium,* teachers do resent this. They say: "We have been trained to instruct pupils in a certain subject. We're not social workers." But in our school, we see that we can only teach the pupils properly when we also do the social work they need.

Q. Your teachers are also required to teach in more than one discipline. . . . What do you think you gain by having teachers teach more than one subject?

A.   More contact between teachers and the students on their teams. For example: Since there are only three classes per team, a teacher who only taught art and music could only teach in his team for twelve periods of his schedule — he would probably have to fill out his schedule by leaving the team for one or two periods a day. He would be torn between the demands of several teams, and he could never develop that close relationship with the students. In contrast, if he also taught German and volunteered for some other assignments—perhaps tutoring or lunchtime activities—he could teach all his twenty-four periods in the team. . . .

Q. Why do teachers prefer it [Team–Small-Group Plan]?

A.   With the team you are not isolated. Your frustration is less because you have colleagues to talk with. You have a place to turn with your teaching problems. The stress is less, the strain is less. And whether you are an adequate teacher or a superior one, you have an opportunity to get better because you can draw on the talent of more experienced teachers.

The teams are simply a very strong backup—if a teacher has personal problems and feels that she can't work as well as she previously had, the team often says, "Relax, we'll do some of your work for a time."

Also, discipline—which is so draining—is less of a problem when you know the students. And actually, we need less preparation time than other teachers. The curriculum conference prepares most materials, and, since we are teaching in just one grade, we may end up with fewer preparations than a counterpart teacher at a traditional school. . . .

Q. I can see how this approach would be a godsend for the average and slower children who are chopped up and worn down in the traditional school. But what about the brightest students? I can see how they might be stifled by this system.

A.   Ironically—though not surprisingly—the studies that have been done show that while all students benefit, the largest gains are made by the brightest. There are several reasons this could be so. One researcher who studied us speculated that the tutoring these top students undertook strengthened their intellectual skills and deepened their understanding. He commented on their diligence in tutoring, noting that if they couldn't help their peers on some task, they would seek out bright kids in other teams to find out how they were teaching it. Also, these students, who might be ostracized and mocked as "eggheads" in another school, are generally valued group members here. There's less pressure for them to conceal their knowledge and talent. Finally, the free learning periods provide an opportunity for them to excel that they might not have elsewhere.

I can tell you that upper-class families that earlier shunned the Comprehensive school in favor of the *Gymnasium* are now eager to enroll their children with us.

Neither CPESS nor Köln-Holweide represents pure forms of *gemeinschaft*. They are, after all, schools and not families or neighborhoods in a literal sense. Nonetheless, both have chosen to organize their lives around a set of values and beliefs that differ quite dramatically from those favored in more traditional schools. They have, in effect, changed their governing theory from formal organization to community. Doing so gives legitimacy to new ways of organizing, new forms of leadership, new patterns of living together and working together, and new practices of teaching and learning.

For example, a common value for CPESS and Köln-Holweide is a commitment to personalized relationships and to caring. This commitment leads both schools to seek ways to become communities of kinship and place. This accounts for their emphasis on continuity. Stanford professor Nel Noddings (1992) discusses the link between caring and continuity:

> To meet the challenge to care in schools, we must plan for continuity:
>
> 1. *Continuity in purpose.* It should be clear that schools are centers of care — that the first purpose is caring for each other. This includes helping all students to address essential issues of human caring and, also, to develop their particular capacities in specialized areas of care.
>
> 2. *Continuity of school residence.* Students should stay in one school building long enough to acquire a sense of belonging. Although I would prefer smaller schools, it may be possible to create a feeling of community in larger schools if community is made a priority. Children should be in resi-

dence more than three and, preferably, for six years.

3. *Continuity of teachers and students.* Teachers, whether singly or in teams, should stay with students (by mutual consent) for three or more years.

4. *Continuity in curriculum.* The idea is to show our care and respect for the full range of human capacities by offering a variety of equally prestigious programs of specialization, each embedded in a universal curriculum organized around essential themes of caring [pp. 72–73].

Community as metaphor for the school is an end in its own right. It yields benefits for schools that are good in and of themselves. But both these schools show that community is also a powerful means to achieve academic ends.

At CPESS students are learning to use their minds well. They know how to learn, to reason, to explore complex problems. They know how to communicate. They are intellectual risk takers. They study math and science throughout their school careers. They score higher than city or state averages on the New York Regency Competency Examinations. In a city, for example, where roughly 40 percent of the students graduate from high school in four years, CPESS graduated 71 percent of its first senior class and 78 percent of its second. Almost all continue their education after graduation.

At Köln-Holweide only 1 percent of the students dropped out in 1988, as compared with the West German average of 14 percent. And 60 percent scored higher on the tough German high school exit exam, which students must pass to qualify for college, compared to the West German average of 21 percent. By any measure this is a formidable record of achievement.

Despite these successes many administrators and teachers remain skeptical. One reason for this skepticism is that critics are evaluating community practices in terms of the old "formal organization" theory. This is the theory that functions in their heads as a mindscape of schooling. Community practices, however, don't make sense unless you change this basic theory. Anne

Ratzki was asked, for example, if other Germans shared her confidence in the Köln-Holweide approach.

> When we first began, many people were skeptical. But by last year, we had 340 applicants for only 220 places. (Despite the growing applicant pool, we still aim for a student body that is mixed according to ability, ethnicity, and sex.) Around the country twenty schools like ours now exist, and many other schools are incorporating pieces of our approach, particularly the pairing of a team of teachers with a particular group of students.
>
> Still it takes a long time for an idea like this to spread. Many superintendents and principals are not too keen on it. But we see that it works for students, that it gives them the strength and support and security they need to succeed in school and in life. So we will continue to use it. As others try it, I think they will see the same, and it will continue to spread [p. 43].

Deborah Meier notes that many visitors to CPESS dismiss what they see by claiming that the school is a special case: "It works in theory but just won't work in the real world of my own backyard." She responds (1991, p. 147):

> People often have a whole string of "well, buts" for why our situation is different from theirs. I want to argue strongly that it is not Deborah Meier, not our unique staff, not extra funds that makes us different. It's our wanting it badly enough. Principals come and say: "Ah, but you have only 500 students. I could do it too if I only had 500." I say, terrific, you can divide your building into a bunch of smaller schools and you too will have schools of only 500. They say: "Well, you have so much more freedom than I do." I remind them that no one actually gave it to me or to us. We have what we took. They say:

"You have an unusual staff." I agree, but it's not because they went to unusual colleges, taught longer, or have exceptional gifts. What's unusual is that they are practicing what they believe in.

It appears that both Anne Ratzki and Deborah Meier have issued us a challenge: Do we have the conviction to give community a try? If the answer is yes, then it's time for us to move on to other dimensions of community building. In the next chapter we examine why community elicits a natural response from people once it is offered.

4

Understanding Our
Need for Community

I believe that once community is offered, we will willingly accept it. Readers might ask, "How can you be sure? Is it really so important that we humans connect with each other? Is it really so important that we identify emotionally with what we do? After all, doesn't community conflict with such traditional values as individual initiative, freedom, choice, and competition?" Underneath, these are questions about what motivates and inspires us, about what we want and need.

In *Moral Leadership* (1992) I suggested that answers to these questions have overplayed the importance of self-interest, personal pleasure, and individual choice and underplayed more altruistic explanations such as our willingness to sacrifice self-interest for purposes and causes we believe in and our propensity to be influenced by membership in groups (gangs, sororities, churches, families, social network, professional associations, neighborhoods, communities, our nation). In that discussion I frequently cited the noted sociologist Amitai Etzioni (1988).

Etzioni challenged the dominance of views of human motivation and decision making that place too much emphasis on rational choice and individual decision making. He pointed out that our emotions, preferences, values, and beliefs and the social bonds with which we identify count too. Granted, it often appears that we are individual decision makers who independently calculate costs and benefits as we seek to maximize our personal gain and minimize our personal losses. But in reality the decisions we make are influenced by norms. We take into account what important others think and believe and how they will react to our decisions. Further, though Etzioni acknowledges that self-interest is important to all of us, we are also capable of selfless behavior. We routinely respond selflessly to felt duties and obligations that emerge from causes and connections we value.

In summarizing that discussion I noted that "what is rewarded gets done" is an important motivational "rule." But it is not the only rule and may not even be the most important one. "What is rewarding gets done" and "what we value and believe to be good gets done" are two others. The first rule motivates through extrinsic gain, the second through intrinsic worth, and the third through felt duties and obligations. The three rules act as extrinsic, intrinsic, and moral ties that have important consequences for how we become involved with each other and how we become attached to our work.

Extrinsic ties lead to calculated involvement. We remain tied to others and to our work as long as we continue to receive and value the rewards that someone else gives us. Intrinsic ties, by contrast, lead to involvement that comes from within. This involvement is inherent in doing something we enjoy and find meaningful. Intrinsic involvement has a way of sustaining itself independently of external factors. Moral ties emerge from the duties we accept and the obligations we feel toward others and toward our work that result from commitments to shared values and beliefs. Moral involvement also comes from within. And, since moral ties are more grounded in cultural norms than psychological gratification, they are likely to be stronger than extrinsic or intrinsic ties.

"What is rewarded gets done" and particularly "what is valued as good gets done" are motivational rules that are underplayed in the management literature. Nonetheless, they are important to the lives of teachers and administrators. In *Moral Leadership* I referred to studies by Dan Lortie (1975) and by Susan Moore Johnson (1990) to illustrate this point. When Lortie asked the teachers in his now-classic Dade County study what attracted them to teaching, the themes that dominated were

serving others, working with other people (particularly students), enjoyment of the job itself, material benefits, and the
school calendar. The dominant themes that emerged from Johnson's research were working with students; an interest in the
intellectual processes, puzzles, problems, and challenges of pedagogy as an occupation; a commitment to learning more or
being more fully engaged in a particular subject area or discipline; social purposes, in the sense of making a difference in
society; religious purposes, in the sense of being called to the
"ministry" of teaching; and a convenient calendar that allowed
combining career with family or with other life interests, mostly
themed to personal development.

Catharine Marshall's recent study of school administrators' values confirms that these themes are alive and well in
the lives of administrators too. In Marshall's words (1992, p. 376):

> During the interviews, the administrators fre-
> quently volunteered statements indicating that
> they saw themselves as ethical administrators and
> moral human beings. When they were asked to talk
> about what guided them when they faced ethical
> dilemmas in their work, . . . the phrase "judgment
> call" kept recurring. . . and they kept referring to
> religion and family background providing guid-
> ance. With no hesitation, many administrators (25
> percent of this sample) talked about guidance from
> God or from their moral principles inculcated by
> church and family. . . . Guthrie said, "Scripture
> guides my decisionmaking." When asked, "What
> guides you in making tough decisions?" Miles said,
> "The heavenly Father. I know that's not the answer
> you're looking for." Easton said, "I do believe that
> God put me into principalship, and from that time
> on I have had nothing but success."

Marshall notes that "the second most prevalent source of
guiding principles was family background and personal values"
(p. 377). And further, "Throughout the interviews, especially in

discussions of situations of conflict, these administrators articu-
lated valuing justice, equity and fairness. Openness, honesty,
and evenhandedness were also dominant themes" (p. 378).

When faced with difficult questions it appears that the
administrators in Marshall's study relied on religious values,
family and personal value systems, their commitment to the
ethic of caring, and their respect for the value of community.
They were motivated by a sense of what was right and good, a
desire to serve others, and a desire to serve ideals. Given these
perspectives it seems safe to conclude that they regularly and
willingly sacrificed their own self-interests on behalf of these
ideals. In this chapter I build upon these ideas by developing a
view of human needs and human nature within the context of
community.

Need theories and practices can be conveniently sorted
into two categories: those that emphasize rational connections
between us and our wants, among us, and between us and our
work, and those that emphasize cultural connections. Rational
and cultural connections parallel the concepts of *gesellschaft* and
gemeinschaft. *Gesellschaft* exists when connections within and
among people are based primarily on the rational pursuit of
self-interest. *Gemeinschaft* exists when connections within and
among people are based primarily on loyalties, purposes, and
sentiments.

We humans are, of course, too complex for our needs,
predispositions, and behaviors to be so easily sorted into just
one of two categories. Both rational and cultural connections
are part of our reality. But the issue is one of primacy. Which of
the categories of thinking best accounts for the nature of human
nature and which should become the overarching framework
for our work as we build community?

Skeptics will point out that the question has already been
answered, that often the behavior of teachers, principals, and
students testifies to calculated involvement, to an emphasis on
self-interest, and to other *gesellschaft* characteristics. My response
is that though many of us are not now responding to cultural
connections, we have the capacity to do so. Nearly all of us had
such a vision when we began our teaching careers. But some-

thing went awry. It appears that our *gesellschaft* experiences in schools changed our initial *gemeinschaft* visions.

Johnson's research suggests that this problem of changing visions may be more acute in public than private schools. She explains: "It seems that there is an important difference between the two kinds of bonds [rational and cultural] described by teachers in this study and the two kinds of social organizations described by Tönnies. Teachers from public and private schools do not seem to differ fundamentally in purpose when they enter teaching; both are compelled by an interest in children, subject matter, and pedagogy. However, once in teaching, schools as organizations seem to shape the experience of one group to resemble *gesellschaft* and the other to resemble *gemeinschaft*" (p. 368).

Johnson defines cultural connections as shared purposes, values, traditions, and history that promote harmony and provide a sense of community. When they are in evidence, we become connected for reason of commitment rather than compliance. Rational connections, by contrast, include roles, role expectations, rules, and functions that are designed to regulate our behaviors. Instead of commitment, compliance is promoted as the way to link people to their work.

Johnson found that private-school teachers were more apt to describe cultural bonds as being prominent in their work. "Compared with their public-school counterparts, they expressed clearer notions of their school's goals and purposes; they identified the values that they shared with others in their schools, they explained how these understandings were grounded in the schools' histories and were reinforced and expressed in their traditions. . . 'faculty here have a clear sense of what this school is hoping to accomplish'" (p. 219). Public-school teachers, by contrast, seldom mentioned cultural bonds, and their schools seemed characterized by "mixed purposes, hazy histories, artificial traditions, and a neutral stance toward values. . . 'I've never felt a strong community sense within the school; I've never felt a strong thing that would pull us all together'" (p. 220).

The issue here is not the capacity of teachers to respond to cultural connections but the willingness of schools to promote them. Though Central Park East Secondary School and the Köln-Holweide school (described in Chapter Three), the Denali School and the Jackson-Keller School (described in Chapters Nine and Ten), and many other public schools are clear exceptions, it appears that private schools seem more at ease with promoting cultural connections. One reason for this may be that it is easier for them to commit to shared purposes — to become communities of mind. Well-established religious and other traditions help them to become communities of memory. Further, they seem more at ease with such *gemeinschaft* relationship characteristics as altruistic love. Public schools, by contrast, often become oversocialized toward the *gesellschaft*, seeing their work less as one of caring and teaching in a "family" sense and one more of diagnosing and instructing in a "professional" sense.

Rational and cultural connections represent competing motivational pulls. On the one hand we want and need community and on the other hand we are socialized to value individualism. In *Habits of the Heart* (1985) Robert Bellah and his colleagues refer to the pulls as two languages, a first language of individualism and a second language of community. Each of the languages represents patterns of thought and behavior we use to find sense and meaning in our lives. The first language of individualism communicates our desire to be independent, indeed detached and autonomous individuals who crave the freedom to define for ourselves our own destiny and to pursue that destiny in our own way, providing that we do not infringe upon the rights of others to do the same thing. The second language of community responds to our innate ability to be connected to each other and to cooperate with each other in pursuit of needs that emerge from a shared conception of our common human nature.

In the ideal the two languages exist in delicate balance. We maintain our sense of privacy and individual freedom while living a cooperative life with others. But Bellah and his colleagues argue that the language of individualism has become so powerful that it seriously threatens the language of community.

The result is lives that become increasingly instrumental, competitive, insulated, and self-seeking. This disconnectedness is evidenced in what freedom often comes to mean to us. "Freedom is perhaps the most resonant, deeply held American value. In some ways, it defines the good in both personal and political life. Yet, freedom turns out to mean being left alone by others, not having other people's values, ideas, or styles of life forced upon one, being free of arbitrary authority and work, family and political life. What it is that one might do with that freedom is much more difficult for Americans to find" (Bellah and others, 1985, p. 23).

Individualism has its merits and demerits. We Americans and Canadians, for example, value self-reliance highly. But we also value self-sufficiency highly and this latter quality can cause problems. Not only do we rely on our own resources, efforts, initiatives, and abilities to get by, we are inclined to provide for our own needs as well. While self-reliance may be a virtue, the press for self-sufficiency often takes on qualities of a perversion. Americans and other Westerners, for example, are prone to seek satisfaction of needs in isolation. As Johan Galtung points out:

> Food is consumed on TV trays, from luncheon boxes, and in "diners"; shelter takes the form of detached houses and apartments away from each other—very different from the clustering in the village as a human habitat; pills and other forms of medication in a sense permit the individuals to treat themselves but also deprive them of social experiences and their connection. . .; machines are more often than not operated by one individual; schooling can be done in loneliness through correspondence courses and "university at a distance"; leisure and recreation are individualized. . .; TV watching in isolation substitutes for secondary and even for primary groups; political activity is reduced to a lonely act of voting in a booth, isolated from the outside; Protestantism and other religious trends define the religious

dimension as a God-individual relation...; telephones reduce communication to a relation between two parties at a time; transportation is in very small units—a car is made for the family at most, a bicycle for the individual; consumer decisions are increasingly made by individuals, not even by families, as women's and children's emancipation get under way. And so on and so forth [1980, p. 95].

The values of self-reliance and self-sufficiency lead us to emphasize individual-dependent need satisfaction, where we rely on ourselves to meet our own needs, and to a lesser extent actor-dependent need satisfaction. In the second case, satisfaction of our needs depends on the motivation and capacity of some other person. When patients, for example, are not able to meet their own needs, physicians meet them. When students are not able to meet their own needs, teachers meet them. When teachers are not able to meet their own needs, principals meet them.

Missing from the equation is structure-dependent need satisfaction, the quality found in communities. It occurs when the capacity for need satisfaction is "built into the social structure itself, as an automatic consequence, not dependent on the motivations and capabilities of particular actors" (Galtung, 1980, p. 64). When we depend on ourselves the "I" looms large. When we depend on another person to meet our needs, the relationship is "I to I." Two people are connected in a contractual way. But when we depend on norms, customs, and mores that are embedded in the social structure itself the "we" looms large. People are bonded to each other as a result of their mutual binding to shared values, traditions, ideas, and ideals.

There is compelling evidence that of the three categories of need satisfaction, we humans are naturally inclined to favor the "we." The "we" is ingrained as part of our human nature. Indeed, this ingraining can be traced back to the very origins of the human species. The seminal work of Louis Leakey and Mary Leakey and later Richard Leakey provides compelling evidence to support this assertion. Richard Leakey and Roger Lewin's book *Origins* (1977) reviews this work. They point out that *homo sapiens sapiens* exhibited trusting relationships and sharing and helping behaviors even before language was developed. They conclude that "humans could not have evolved in the remark-able way in which we undoubtedly have unless our ancestors were strongly cooperative creatures. The key to the transforma-tion of a social ape-like creature into a cultural animal living in a highly structured and organized society is sharing; the sharing of jobs and the sharing of food" (pp. 10–11). They continue, "We are essentially cultural animals with the capacity to formulate many kinds of social structures; but a deep-seated biological urge towards cooperation, towards working as a group, provides a basic framework for these structures" (p. 223).

Andrew Oldenquist (1991) notes that there is growing scientific evidence to support the thesis that "humans evolved to be innately social animals, to be tribal creatures and group egotists who are emotionally dependent on group membership and who are discontented and function poorly in environments that are too individualistic" (p. 92). He states further, "We should be ready to explore the idea that the emotions our Pleistocene ancestors evolved come back to haunt us, that we are genetically predisposed to need to live (and be brought up in) certain ways, within certain limits as socialized creatures, and that we feel insecure, aimless, and hostile when we are denied these limits" (p. 96). He argues that it is in our nature to be social animals, "to be socialized and brought up belonging to and caring about the good of our families, clans, tribes, towns, or countries" (p. 107). This "group egoism," as he refers to it, is essential to our human being and its absence causes alienation. Many children—too many—could not "be reared in a way more antithetical to the development of sense of belonging, social morality, personal responsibility, work ethic, and a sense of engaging in useful and meaningful activity" (p. 97). Schools alone can't fix the problems of society. Schools alone cannot mend community where com-munity is broken. But schools can provide substitutes by becom-ing communities themselves.

Readers who feel more comfortable with the creation theory as the literal explanation of our origins can take comfort.

The Bible too stands as testimony to our communal nature, our need for community. Thus, both theories lead to the same inescapable conclusion.

Durkheim's Theory of Needs

The famous French sociologist Emile Durkheim proposed that we humans have a basic need to belong, to be connected to each other, and to identify with a set of norms that gives direction and meaning to our lives. In *The Division of Labor in Society* ([1893] 1964) he introduced the concept of *anomie* to help explain this need. As Schweitzer (1991) points out, *anomie* derives from the Greek word *nomos*, which refers to customs and traditions that are embodied in mores, values, goals, and norms. The prefix *a* means "without." Durkheim's basic thesis was that when we are without mores, values, goals, and norms we become alienated from ourselves, from others, and ultimately from society, with all of the imaginable negative consequences.

One danger of emphasizing *gesellschaft* over *gemeinschaft* in schools and in other institutions is that it can lead to *anomie*. For Durkheim, the antidote was community. Community is a basic need that, when unmet, contributes to *anomie*. Key to his understanding of community was the concept of collective conscience, defined as collective moral awareness, mutual obligation, and involvement in a collectivity. In Durkheim's theory, involvement in community has three elements: duty, attachment, and self-determination. Drawing on Durkheim's writings, Schweitzer (pp. 76–77) summarizes the three as follows:

1. Discipline [duty], implying a sense of self-constraint through duty to the collectivity
2. Attachment, involving a sense of membership, commitment and identity with the collectivity
3. Personal autonomy or self-determination, involving knowledge, understanding, and a rational sense of awareness regarding the reasons for discipline [duty] and attachment to the collectivity

In sum, Durkheim proposes that community is a basic human need. Community can be understood as collective conscience, which is composed of three moral elements: duty, attachment, and self-determination. When the collective conscience is lost, we are deprived of opportunities to respond to duty, to become attached, to express self-determination. When this happens we experience *anomie*; a sense of normlessness and disconnectedness.

If we are not willing to settle for *anomie*, we are inclined to search for substitutes. One substitute is to create an artificial collective conscience. Students, for example, turn to themselves and insulate themselves from the school and the adult world it represents by creating strong student subcultures. At the extreme, they turn to gangs. Teachers create an artificial collective conscience by turning to informal groups that represent a marginal, albeit powerful, life within the formal life of the school. When students and teachers turn to alternative sources, duty, attachment, and self-determination can become defined as dysfunctional norm systems designed to resist change, to discourage cooperation, and to disconnect them from others and from their work.

Revisiting Basic-Needs Theories

Basic-needs theories remain fundamental to the way we think about needs and the way we think about motivation in schools, but they are not without controversy. One issue is the extent to which any given list of basic needs is universally applicable as opposed to being culturally bound. A given set of needs, for example, might make sense in parts of the United States and Canada but not in parts of Africa, South America, or Asia. What makes sense to African Americans or to Native Canadians may not make sense to other groups.

One way to mediate the universal versus cultural controversy is to differentiate more clearly between basic needs and need satisfiers. Food, for example, is a universal need, but how that need is satisfied is culturally determined. Gilbert Rist (1980) believes that needs must be understood within the context of their potential satisfiers. It is not enough to say that one must eat; we must also take into account what will be eaten, with whom, when, and why. "Food alone, then, cannot be taken as the 'satisfier' of the 'need,'" Rist comments. "For example, will a committed Muslim satisfy the need for food by eating pork with a woman? . . . People almost never eat just to be fed, but also to communicate with others (to share bread and salt, bread and wine, etc.). A meal is a way of understanding and organizing relationships with both the natural and social environment. This is also why people in many societies prefer to live below the minimum level. . . in order to 'waste' in feasts, sacrifices, cere- monies, and the like" (p. 237).

Similarly, the need to belong can be satisfied in a number of ways. In our society students naturally satisfy this need through family, neighborhood, friendship, school, and commu- nity ties. When these satisfiers are not available, they search elsewhere. The greater the array of acceptable satisfiers the less likely that unacceptable ones will be chosen.

Still another issue is whether value should be placed on one need as opposed to another. My own research and writings over the years, for example, assumed that a hierarchy of needs existed. Within this hierarchy some needs were thought to be "basic" and others were thought to be "higher" (Sergiovanni, 1967; Sergiovanni and Carver, 1980). But this kind of thinking causes problems. Abraham Maslow's theory of motivation is a good example. The needs he described are typically arranged in a pyramid composed of five levels ascending from physiological, to safety, to belonging, to self-esteem, and finally to self- actualization. Whether intended by Maslow or not, self-esteem and self-actualization are generally considered to be higher- order needs and thus more valued than the other three. Further, there is an assumption that to find true fulfillment one must climb the ladder of needs to the top, further reinforcing the notion that those at the top are more important than those at the bottom.

As a result of this kind of thinking, there is a tendency to devalue needs of belonging, which is only midway up the ladder. We tend to see them as some sort of irritant that needs fixing so that people will be free to focus on more important things such as achievement and success. One consequence of this devaluing is to create a view of school administration that prizes strong leadership and achievement over caring leadership and nurturance.

Certainly Maslow did not intend such devaluing. He considered belonging to be critical to our being, less a means to climb to the "next rung" and more an end in itself. In his words, "We have very little scientific information about the belongingness need, although this is a common theme in novels, autobiographies, poems and plays and also in the newer psychological literature. From these we know in a general way the destructive effects on children of moving too often; of disorientation; of the general over-mobility that is forced by industrialization; of being without roots, or of despising one's roots, one's origins, one's group; of being torn from one's home and family, and friends and neighbors; of being a transient or a newcomer rather than a native. We still underplay the deep importance of the neighborhood, of one's territory, of one's clan, of one's own 'kind,' one's class, one's gang, one's familiar working colleagues. . . . [We have, in effect] unsatisfied hunger for contact, for intimacy, for belongingness and for the need to overcome the widespread feelings of alienation, aloneness, strangeness and loneliness, which have been worsened by our mobility, by the breakdown of traditional groupings, the scattering of families, the generation gap, the steady urbanization and disappearance of village face-to-faceness, and the resulting shallowness of American friendship" (1970, p. 43).

Another famous psychologist, Eric Erickson, didn't devalue the need to belong either. He believed that belonging provides us with the identity we need to function successfully as individuals. Our personal development, he argued, presupposed identity with a community of people (Erickson, 1966). Among African Americans, Latino Americans, and Native Americans, for example, the need to belong is highly valued. Citing Nobles's 1973 research, Klineberg (1980) points out that the Eurocentric view is that "the self is individually unique and different from ourselves. The African world view, on the other hand, suggests that 'I am because we are, and because we are, therefore I am'" (p. 25). Standing Bear (1933) pointed out that in traditional native communities belonging is so valued that responsibility for it transcends the family. Native children, for example, were raised in a tribal setting by a network of caretakers.

This "we" orientation predominates on the surface in more traditional non-Western societies. Underneath the surface, however, it is important to all of us. Belonging may free us to climb to the next level of needs, but it is first and foremost an end in itself—a way, according to Maslow, that we find meaning and significance in our lives and a way, according to Erickson, that we strengthen our own personal identities. It appears that healthy "I's" depend upon healthy "we's."

Popular interpretations of Maslow's needs hierarchy often make belonging needs conditional rather than guaranteed. In order for students to be accepted and loved, for example, they need to comply by obeying the rules and to achieve by learning what the teacher asks them to learn. Failing either of these, they are rejected. Sometimes the rejection is psychological. At other times it is both psychological and physical: students who do not comply and who do not achieve are isolated from others.

Norman Kunc refers to this phenomenon as the inversion of Maslow's hierarchy. In his words, "It is not uncommon for educators to work from the premise that *achievement and mastery rather than belonging are the primary if not the sole precursors of self-esteem*. . . . The current education system, in fact, has dissected and inverted Maslow's hierarchy of needs so that belonging has been transformed from an unconditional need and right of all people into something that must be earned, something that can be achieved only by the 'best' of us" (1992, p. 381). He continues, "The curricula and the structure of our schools are based on the assumption that children who come to school have had their psychological and safety needs met at home. Students, upon entering school, are immediately expected to learn the curriculum. Successful mastery of schoolwork is expected to foster the children's sense of self-worth, which in turn will enable them to join the community as 'responsible citizens.' Children are required, as it were, to *learn* their right to belong" (p. 31).

Schools have important roles to play as arenas and contexts for the fulfillment of human needs. For adults our work can be either a source of satisfaction or merely a way to earn a living. The stakes are even higher for students. In a society where loss of community seems real, schools become an important place, for some the only place, where students' needs are met. Which conception of schooling holds the greatest promise for filling the needs of its members—the *gesellschaft* school, conceived as formal organization, or the *gemeinschaft* school, conceived as community?

Table 4.1 can help us answer this question. John Galtung (1980, p. 66) has created a list of basic needs divided into four broad categories: security, welfare, identity, and freedom. To the right of the needs is a column labeled "satisfiers." To use this system in our thinking about schools, try to think of a relevant satisfier for each need that can be found in schools conceived as organizations, then think of a relevant satisfier that can be found in schools conceived as communities.

In some cases the satisfiers will be the same. For nutrition (a welfare need) both school-as-organization and school-as-community provide lunch programs. In other cases the satisfiers will be different. Students have a need to be safe from violence. In organizations, students are protected by beefing up security and by issuing rules that regulate the movement and assembly of students. Schools as communities are also concerned about these things. But at the heart they rely on providing substitutes for gangs, substitutes that become more constructive satisfiers for the need to belong. Some categories of needs will be just as easily met in either organization or community. This is the case for the welfare needs. Other categories will favor one image of schooling over another. Identity needs and freedom needs, for example, are more easily met in schools understood as communities than in schools understood as organizations.

The value of community is an end in itself that requires no further justification. But schools are special kinds of communities. They are learning communities and that makes them

Table 4.1. Basic Needs and Potential Satisfiers.

	Satisfiers	
Basic Need	In Communities	In Organization
Security needs (survival needs) — *to avoid violence*	————	————
Against individual violence (assault, torture)	————	————
Against collective violence (wars, internal, external)	————	————
Welfare needs (sufficiency needs) — *to avoid misery*	————	————
For nutrition, water, air, sleep	————	————
For movement, excretion	————	————
For protection against climate, environment	————	————
For protection against diseases	————	————
For protection against excessive strain	————	————
For self-expression, dialogue, education	————	————
Identity needs (needs for closeness) — *to avoid alienation*	————	————
For self-expression, creativity, praxis, work	————	————
For self-actuation, for realizing potentials	————	————
For well-being, happiness, joy	————	————
For being active and subject; not being passive, client, object	————	————
For challenge and new experiences	————	————
For affection, love, sex; friends, spouse, offspring	————	————
For roots, belongingness, support, esteem; association with similar humans	————	————
For understanding social forces; for social transparence	————	————
For partnership with nature	————	————
For a sense of purpose, of meaning with life; closeness to the transcendental, transpersonal	————	————
Freedom needs (freedom to; choice, option) — *to avoid repression*	————	————
Choice in receiving and expressing information and opinion	————	————
Choice of people and places to visit and be visited	————	————
Choice in consciousness formation	————	————
Choice in mobilization	————	————
Choice in confrontation	————	————
Choice of occupation	————	————
Choice of place to live	————	————
Choice of spouse	————	————
Choice of goods and services	————	————
Choice of way of life	————	————

Source: Galtung, 1980, p. 66. Used by permission.

purposeful communities as well. They are responsible for providing students with successful, academically challenging experiences. Thankfully, building community is also a means to promoting such success. In a way, we care to learn, and that smacks of *gesellschaft*. But at the heart of it, we learn *because* we care and that is clearly *gemeinschaft*.

5

Becoming a
Purposeful Community

Schools can become communities in many different forms. They
can become:

- Caring communities where members, motivated by altruistic love, make a total commitment to each other and where
  the characteristics that define their relationships are clearly
  gemeinschaft
- Learning communities where members are committed to
  thinking, growing, and inquiring and where learning is for
  everyone an attitude as well as an activity, a way of life as well
  as a process
- Professional communities where members make a commitment to the continuous development of their expertise and
  to the ideals of professional virtue
- Collegial communities where members are tied together for
  mutual benefit and to pursue common goals by a sense of
  felt interdependence and mutual obligation
- Inclusive communities where economic, religious, cultural,
  ethnic, family, and other differences are brought together
  into a mutually respectful whole
- Inquiring communities where principals and teachers commit themselves to a spirit of collective inquiry as they reflect
  on their practice and search for solutions to the problems
  they face

But to be any of these, schools must first become purposeful communities. They must become places where mem-

bers have developed a community of mind that bonds them together in special ways and binds them to a shared ideology. Schools cannot become caring communities, for example, unless caring is valued and unless norms are created that point the way toward caring, reward caring behaviors, and frown on noncaring behaviors. Nor can schools become learning communities, professional communities, collegial communities, inclusive communities, or inquiring communities without valuing these respective images and without developing norm systems that guide their quest for community.

The culture of a school arises from a network of shared ideologies, coherent sets of beliefs that tie people together and that explain their work to them in terms of cause and effect relationships (Trice and Beyer, 1984). Ideologies are the means by which we make sense of our lives, find direction, and commit ourselves to courses of action. In communities, ideologies shape what principals and teachers believe and how they practice. They influence, as well, what students believe and how they behave. Emergent courses of action, in turn, communicate and affirm meanings that ensure what we do is both purposeful and sensible. Ideologies are antidotes to loss of community and resulting feelings of *anomie*. Networks of shared ideologies represent a community of mind upon which to build communities of kinship, place, and memory.

Where does one begin the process of becoming a purposeful community? One popular strategy is for schools to identify and commit to "core values." Newton, Massachusetts, school superintendent Irwin Blumer believes that "Core Values are not just concepts to speak or write about. These values affect the way people think and feel and behave. The Core Values which a group selects as its own should be so significant that they permeate every aspect of the school organization. Every decision that is made in the school system should reflect the commitment to these principles. Should a member of the school community violate a Core Value, there is an immediate and strong reaction to that violation. Core Values define the purposes of the school. Just as importantly, they define and unify the school system" (Newton Public Schools, 1992, p. 1).

The Newton Public Schools function on the basis of three core values (pp. 2–3):

1. *Centrality of the classroom.* The most important learning in a school occurs in classroom interaction between a teacher and students. The Newton Public Schools recognize the importance of classroom teachers and will support and empower them in their efforts to ensure that all children learn to their fullest potential. The culture of the Newton schools will ensure that the voice of the teacher is heard on all issues that impact on the classroom experience.

2. *Respect for human differences.* The strength of our nation resides in the diversity which exists in the country. The Newton Public Schools support teachers as they seek to provide a rich environment for teaching and learning, where adults and children gain knowledge and respect for different races, religions, nationalities, and cultures, within our school system, community and the world.

3. *Support for collegial behavior.* An educational environment must provide formal and informal structures which expect and encourage teachers to work together. These structures enable teachers to learn more about the craft of teaching, as well as provide opportunities to reflect upon their practice and to gain support for innovation.

At both the district level and the level of each individual school, the Newton School District designs out from these values as it creates school structures, develops policies, identifies goals, translates the goals into "core outcomes," makes decisions about how they will treat each other and work together, decides what to teach and how to teach, and plans for evaluation. Each year, for example, Blumer meets with the Newton school committee to discuss and approve a set of systemwide goals for the year. The goals are always organized around the three core values.

During the 1991–92 school year, for example, eight broad goals and nineteen subgoals were identified. With respect to centrality of the classroom (core value 1) the Newton Public Schools made the following commitments:

- To create a culture that supports teachers as reflective decision makers on instruction.
- To support and involve teachers in the ongoing process of curriculum development, review, and revision.
- To establish opportunities for teachers to provide input and be informed and involved in decision making on school-based and system-wide policies and procedures.

These commitments led to the establishment of the following goals:

Continue to support study groups, mentoring programs, grade-level meetings, faculty senates, and other activities that bring teachers together to focus on, discuss, and share effective classroom instructional strategies.

Develop a process of decision making which ensures that the voice of the teacher is heard on issues that directly impact on the classroom experience.

Strive to protect classroom instructional time by limiting and/or carefully planning necessary interruptions.

Continue to encourage and provide for teacher participation and leadership in school-year curriculum development and summer curriculum projects.

Provide opportunities for teachers to take full advantage of curriculum materials through systemwide dissemination of successful strategies and practices.

Provide opportunities for teachers to share their skills and expertise as presenters in curriculum dissemination workshops and other forms within and beyond the system.

Ensure that teachers are informed in a timely manner of issues of policy and procedure which impact them.

Ensure teacher input is solicited and considered before decisions are made.

Ensure the timely communication of decisions along with rationales.

Commitments made for the values of respect for human differences and support for collegial behavior were:

- To provide effective, challenging and creative instruction which is responsive to different learning styles. Respect for human differences places the learner in the center of the classroom and fashions instruction which builds upon the learner's unique strengths and addresses his/her needs.
- To identify and integrate information which celebrates the contributions of all people to the development of society.
- To protect the integrity of the curriculum by ensuring constant and thorough input and feedback from teachers.
- To make collegial behavior a thematic priority which builds mutual trust and cooperation among teachers and administrators; and to validate and reward collegial behavior when it occurs [pp. 1–6].

These commitments led to the establishment of still other goals.

For Newton, the three core values serve as powerful value pillars for each of the individual schools in the district. District commitments and goals provide direction and parameters within which individual schools must work. Every school, for example, is required to prepare a development plan that highlights important initiatives it hopes to take each year. Principals and teachers work together on the plan. What is to be done, and how, are matters of individual school choice, providing the core values are addressed.

In Newton, schools are tightly connected to values but loosely connected to how these values will be embodied. Two empowerment rules seem to be operating: schools are free to do what makes sense to them providing the decisions they make embody the district's core values; and, within each school, teachers, principals, and others are free to do what makes sense to them providing that the decisions they make embody the values that are shared by the school (Sergiovanni, 1991).

Blumer describes this tight–loose connectedness as follows: "One elementary school may choose, under 'Centrality of the Classroom,' to examine its reading program, including materials, staff training, library resources, parental involvement, diagnostic testing, etc. Another may choose to seek changes in its science program. Still another may elect to concentrate on cooperative learning approaches to teaching. The active involvement of staff members in the school is basic to this process. Under 'Respect for Human Differences,' one school may concentrate on expanding the involvement of a growing Hispanic population in the school; while another focuses on greater use of literature to enhance multi-cultural education. Establishing a study group, supported by the system but carried on at the building level, is one way to implement 'Collegial Behavior,' but schools may identify other approaches" (Newton Public Schools, 1992, p. 4). Blumer adds: "Individual schools in Newton have a long history of autonomy. Principals select their own staff and determine how their budgets are spent. Schools are organized differently within the system. Teaching styles differ; teachers select their own materials and often develop their own curricula. What unifies the schools and creates the school system, as opposed to nineteen ships sailing in many different directions, is our commitment to specific core values. No matter what school you enter in Newton, you will see evidence of work to address these values" (p. 5).

A strength of Newton's approach is its realization that professionalism and community building at the individual school level depend upon the sense of community that is developed districtwide. This realization is consistent with recent research on the topic. Stanford professor Milbrey McLaughlin (1992) explains: "The character of the professional community created at the district level. . . directly affects teachers' commitment to their profession and sense of professional worth; district level community indirectly influenced teachers' learning and commitment to their students and their own professional growth by way of the broader context it established for the school workplace" (p. 9).

A goal for the 1991–92 school year was to push the strategy of designing out from values deep into the Newton School District. All nineteen schools were invited to identify their own core values from which they might better organize themselves for teaching and learning. They were invited, in other words, to become individual communities of mind, united together into a Newton School District community of mind. Blumer explains, "Using the concept of Core Values at the building level is critically important. Nothing is as powerful as the process that brings together the principal, staff and parent community to reach consensus on the Core Values of a particular school. . . . The development of Core Values at the school level provides a structure within which staff members and parents can reach agreement on what they want the school to emphasize and accomplish. Once children understand that there is common agreement on important values at both home and school, the school can much more readily build a sense of commitment within the student body" (Newton Public Schools, 1992, p. 9).

With the help of John Saphier, president of Research for Better Schools, and John D'Auria, principal of Wellesley Middle School, a designing-out-from-values initiative was started throughout the district. Saphier provided the following guidelines for deciding whether a value is really a value.

- The value permeates the school and drives its decision.
- There is a strong reaction when the value is violated and it is among the last things that one gives up.
- Schools were required to involve parents and teachers and to reach a consensus on its values.

The Angier School began to identify its core values by meeting with parents on November 14, 1991. The following letter from the principal reports the progress of that meeting (Chapman, 1991):

November 18, 1991

Dear Parents,

On Thursday evening, we began a process by which we would define what you and staff most want your child to gain from his or her experiences at Angier School.

The topic was entitled "Core Values." As we held our discussions and summations, I began to feel that the topic would be better explained as "Core Outcomes." We should think in terms of answering the following questions:

1. What are the three or four most important things we want our children to have learned in their years at our school?
2. What do we want our children to carry away with them, perhaps for the rest of their lives, that might not have happened without the systematic attention we all paid to it?
3. If we could give our child(ren) a gift that could not be purchased or wrapped, but a gift that could ensure he or she would develop along the lines of our deepest hopes, what would that gift be?

Several core outcomes [values] which I heard Thursday evening were:

•   to foster a love of learning—that is, to be life-long learners.
•   to provide an environment which is safe intel-

lectually and emotionally to take risks, to see mistakes as opportunity not as failures.

- to understand and respect cultural diversity.
- to feel that school, home, and community are safe.
- to have a feeling of self-fulfillment and happiness.
- to develop the ability to challenge their own beliefs — to change their minds based on new experiences or knowledge.
- to know how to learn.

If you didn't have a chance to come and give input, I invite you to do so and to send a note to me care of the Angier Office.

Sincerely,
Ruth W. Chapman

Several other meetings were held to further discuss and refine the values. Angier decided to begin the process by having parents develop one list of core values and teachers another. In March of 1992 parents and teachers met together to combine, clarify, refine, and classify the values.

The strategy adopted by the Newton schools to become purposeful communities resembles the popular outcomes-based education (OBE) movement. Though designing out from values and OBE strategies share some characteristics, they are not the same. The OBE approach typically requires the identification and specification of measurable student performance outcomes. These outcomes (often called "exit outcomes") are competencies that students must demonstrate before completing a particular lesson, unit, course, or school year. Completion, in some cases, is a requirement for graduation. Instead of emphasizing *designing out* from values, OBE emphasizes *designing down* from performance outcomes. According to Spady, OBE means "organizing for results: basing what we do instructionally on the outcomes we want to achieve" (1988, p. 5).

Outcomes-based education offers a number of advantages. Prime among them is that the strategy is inclusive. Advocates firmly believe that all students can learn and will learn given the right (that is, OBE) circumstances. OBE, for example, is often accompanied by mastery learning as an instructional process. Mastery learning begins with identifying well-defined learning objectives. Well-organized learning units that are closely aligned with these objectives are then constructed. Monitoring systems are often developed to be sure that teachers teach the prescribed curriculum. The curriculum is then taught directly by teachers. Tests are used to determine the extent to which students have achieved the objectives. Throughout, students are provided with regular feedback, guidance, and direction, not only to let them know what they must learn and how, but to provide them with whatever extra help they might need to master the material. Usually time is not an issue. Students are allowed as much time as they need to master the material. To Spady, OBE "means having all students learn well, not just the fastest, the brightest, or the most advantaged" (p. 4).

Despite this commitment to inclusiveness in learning, the OBE strategy can present some problems. OBE is linear — curriculum is designed down from performance outcomes. But sound curriculum choices and decisions about effective teaching and learning practices are anything but linear. They are as likely to emerge *in use* as teachers practice, as they are to be set beforehand. Further, teachers are not just concerned with instructional objectives and outcomes but other kinds as well.

Relying only on instructional objectives or outcomes implies that all knowledge is certain and can be laid out in sequence; that all knowledge is absolute with only one answer being appropriate; and that all knowledge is impersonal and therefore the same for all (MacDonald and Wolfson, 1970). In the real world whatever is taught is filtered through and mediated by the personal meanings that learners bring to the setting, and this contributes to a kind of unpredictability in terms of outcomes. Also, good teachers are opportunists who, within broad guidelines, embark on a journey whose happy ending is often hard to determine beforehand. They are concerned as much, if not more, about the quality of individual learning encounters (regardless of preset objectives) than they are about engineering learning encounters from preset objectives. They are concerned, in other words, with *expressive* objectives and outcomes.

The widely respected curriculum theorist Elliot Eisner explains, "Expressive objectives [outcomes] differ considerably from instructional objectives. An expressive objective does not specify the behavior the student is to acquire after having engaged in one or more learning activities. An expressive objective describes an educational encounter: It identifies a situation in which children are at work, a problem with which they are to cope, a task that they are to engage in—but it does not specify the form of that encounter, situation, problem, or task they are to learn. An expressive objective provides both the teacher and the student with an invitation to explore, defer or focus on issues that are of peculiar interest or import to the inquirer" (1969, pp. 15–16).

Since OBE learning outcomes are typically universal and always set beforehand, students often have very little to say about what they will learn. Thus, the outcomes do not always reflect unique characteristics and interests of all students. Further, once the curriculum is aligned to the outcomes, teachers are required to teach directly to them. This process includes frequent measuring of the extent to which outcomes are being reached and reteaching as necessary until the outcomes are mastered.

In a sense, the outcomes and the linear chain of events that follow can become scripts that limit the decisions teachers make. Once outcomes are set by the school, teachers are not free to select their own. Initially, they may have autonomy over means, but this autonomy may be elusive. Over time, choices as to what to teach, when, and how can become increasingly limited by the outcomes toward which one must teach.

Advocates of outcomes-based education claim that it is not a package but a process designed to help schools decide what to teach, how, and when. Whether OBE remains a process once implementation is under way, or becomes a package, depends on the instructional model that accompanies the overall philosophy. When performance objectives are tightly linked to curriculum choices and curriculum choices are tightly linked to teaching strategies, monitoring, and testing, the OBE process is in danger of becoming a package, whether intended or not. And when this happens, teacher discretion is narrowed, translating in less-effective learning experiences for students and endangering the development of professional community. OBE combined with an alignment instructional model risks resembling a funnel:

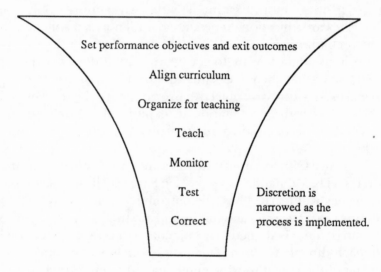

Set performance objectives and exit outcomes

Align curriculum

Organize for teaching

Teach

Monitor

Test

Correct

Discretion is narrowed as the process is implemented.

The problem is more serious when curriculum choices are made beforehand and considered to be standard imperatives for all teachers to follow. The problem is less serious when curriculum choices are made *in use* as teachers and teams of teachers actually teach. Different teachers, in this case, are free to make different choices if they feel the need to do so.

Even if the OBE model allowed for teacher discretion over means in practice, we have to ask if this discretion is enough. Too often, for example, we tell teachers that we *don't care* how they get kids to meet outcomes. Noddings (1992) relates a story where a superintendent did just that. "'You can stand them on their heads in the back of the room for all I care, [he told the teachers] but perform they must.' His teachers knew the superintendent was not totally serious in his neglect of means, but he seemed too serious for his conscientious teachers. They saw teaching as a moral enterprise, not one in which the end justifies the means. Ostensibly they were free to use their professional judgment in choosing instructional means, but they were forbidden to tamper with the ends. Such constraint is not the mark of a professional, and these teachers resented it" (p. 7).

Virtually all the problems associated with OBE can be lessened by disconnecting "exit outcomes" from tightly aligned instructional models and by linking them instead to values that address more fully the entire array of school issues. Borrowing a leaf from the quality guru W. Edward Deming (1986), if we focus on values first and then the processes that are consistent with these values, outcome specifics will take care of themselves. If we followed this advice, OBE would become less instrumental. A clear distinction would no longer be made between means and ends. Both would be valued as ends, which would make the OBE strategy less *gesellschaft* and more *gemeinschaft*, thus further strengthening the development of community.

The Coalition of Essential Schools, for example, rallies its efforts around a set of values that are shared by its members. As Sizer points out, "Our approach is an approach of ideas; we have shared commitments, not shared things. Our ideas will inform a way as guideposts, not as hitching posts. We allow our priorities to be driven by our ideas seriously because we're serious about kids" (Jefferson County Public Schools, 1991).

The Coalition values are summarized as follows: the school should focus on helping students use their minds well; school goals should be simple, with each student mastering a number of essential skills and being competent in certain areas of knowledge; schools' goals should apply to all students but the means to these goals should vary; teaching and learning should be personalized; the governing metaphor of the school should be student as worker; the diploma should be awarded based on the successful demonstration of mastery exhibitions; the tone of the school should stress the values of unanxious expectation, of trust, and of decency; principals and teachers should view themselves as generalists first and then as specialists; and teachers should be provided with substantial time for collective planning (Sizer, 1992).

Certainly there are hints of "exit outcomes" in this statement of values. But the statement transcends an enumeration of what students are expected to do by creating a set of conceptions that govern the lives of all those involved and that affect every aspect of the life of the school, not just what is taught at ten o'clock on Monday morning. For example, the Coalition of Essential Schools values, combined with their deep commitment to professional autonomy, led teachers at Central Park East Secondary School (described in Chapter Three) to rebuild the traditional school structure. Prime in their minds was to find ways to give teachers more time to know each student well and more time to tailor teaching for personalized learning. To get the job done, they had to be interested in a lot more than just listing exit outcomes. Here are examples of what they felt they had to do.

Time for Students
- To get the student load way down, all professional staff—including the librarian and the director—teach. Aside from one director, there are no supervisors.
- The high school is organized into houses of eighty students, each with a faculty of four. The basic class is twenty students and the student load per teacher is never more than eighty. If the teacher teaches two disciplines instead of one, the load is just forty.
- To maximize the personal relationship between students and teachers, students stay with the same teacher (or teachers) two years in a row.

Time for Teachers
- Each fall the staff plans a series of semimonthly faculty meetings. One year, every other faculty meeting considered various approaches to writing. Sometimes, at a teacher's request, one student's progress or one teacher's curriculum is discussed.
- Once a week, the staff of each house takes an eighty-minute

lunch and discusses the progress of individual students and the overall work of the house.

- One morning a week, while students work in the community, teachers from each department can spend three uninterrupted hours designing, evaluating, and tinkering with the curriculum.

The Curriculum
- The curriculum is designed by those who teach it. Teachers can opt to hire consultants.
- The seventh- and eighth-grade science sequence includes an interdisciplinary unit on "Light and Sight" that exposes students to both biology (optics) and physics (the properties of light).
- The eighth-grade humanities sequence focuses on power — who has it, who doesn't, and how different people have gotten it. The first semester focuses on the English, French, and American revolutions; the second, on nonrevolutionary change in America.

Flexible Scheduling
- Because the schedule is in the hands of teachers, the time allotted to teaching the revolutions could be increased when it was discovered that at least one student still thought Boston was in London.

Resources
- Once a topic, such as the revolutions, has been chosen, all faculty haunt used-book shops to build a resource library on the subject. Teachers are thus not textbound but have access to a variety of materials, some of which will interest every student.

Writing
- Working in different settings with different "editors," students get plenty of practice with — and individual attention to — their writing. They write at least once a week in humanities and in a "writing workshop," plus four days a week in regularly reviewed journals.

Parent Conferences

• Twice a year, parents must come to the school, review a portfolio of their child's work, and meet with the teacher *and* the student to discuss the student's progress. With everybody in the same room together, parent's won't hear one version of events from the student and another from the teacher (McPike, 1987, p. 37).

James G. Henderson (1992) recommends "clustering" as a means to begin the process of designing out from values. Let's suppose that two of the values that a particular school is committed to are "being inquiring and reflective teachers" and "making teacher professionalism work for us." A first step in identifying what these values mean to the everyday lives of community members might be for each teacher to share thoughts and ideas that come to mind as they reflect on the values. They might do this by creating cluster diagrams as shown in Figures 5.1 and 5.2. The cluster diagrams could then be used to enlarge the conversation, as teachers share their thoughts and construct a collective cluster diagram.

Expeditionary Learning — Community in the Making

To create community, start with an ideology, a set of conceptions about what schools are for, what is good for students, what makes sense about teaching and learning, and how everyone involved should live their lives together. Start, in other words, by developing a community of mind. Next, invite others to join this community of mind, relying on the persuasiveness of compelling ideas. Leave plenty of room for those who join to shape their own destiny while being informed by the key values. Help them to create their own school communities — communities of kinship and communities of place. This is what a group of people decided to do when they responded to the New American Schools Development Corporation's request for proposals to create new designs for schools.

Dubuque, Iowa, superintendent Diana Lam served as principal designer of the proposal, working with a team that

Figure 5.1. Cluster Diagram on "Teaching Professionalism."

Source: Henderson, 1992, p. 162. Used by permission.

Figure 5.2. Cluster Diagram on Being an "Inquiring, Reflective Teacher."

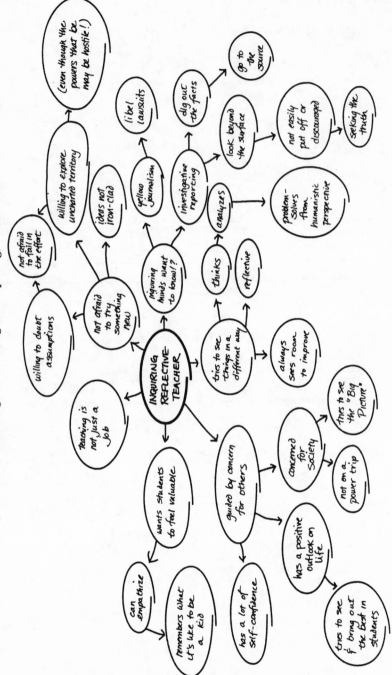

Source: Henderson, 1992, p. 34. Used by permission.

included Greg Farrell of Outward Bound U.S.A., representatives from such organizations as the Academy for Educational Development, Educators for Social Responsibility, Facing History, Facing Ourselves, a contingent of people from the Harvard Graduate School of Education, and others. Their proposal, "Expeditionary Learning: A Design for New American Schools," was one of 11 funded from a field of 686.

> Our design is based upon a shared set of principals. These are our "givens." As articulated by Harvard dean emeritus Paul Ylvisaker: "Values must be clear and the value of values clearly demonstratable; there is no learning without emotion and challenge; it must be done with intimacy and caring; the collective and the individual can be brought together, there must be a fair assurance of success." Harvard professor Eleanor Duckworth has called attention to the spirit of infectious intellectual excitement and inquiry; and [Outward Bound founder] Kurt Hahn's work and writings insists on our final guiding principles: the importance of solitude and reflection; and the need to develop community and social vision ["Expeditionary Learning," 1992, p. 3].

The proposers use the metaphor "expeditionary learning" as the central organizing concept for their school. It includes the broad range of intelligences and relationships that are necessary to complete challenging intellectual and experiential expeditions. These "expeditions are discovery operations. They start from scratch and travel light, relying on courage and compassion as much as intellectual and physical acumen. They go somewhere, but the place is new, at least to every participant. They demand teamwork and the personal best from members to achieve success. They also require a high level of competence on the part of expedition guides" (p. ii).

The proposers provide a set of principles to guide the design process as expeditionary learning schools are created.

The process is one of designing out from values. The design principles are as follows:

> *The value of values:* "Unless thinking and values connect vitally with the continuum of experience in human lives, the ideas quickly become disembodied, unthinking, inhuman. People lose sight of who they are and what their roots are. . . . Every step forward in intellectual growth should be accompanied by a strengthening of moral perspective and a more fully activated life of learning in pursuit of human ends. Every word and symbol, each gesture that makes meaning, the entire tree of knowledge must send its taproot down into this reality: We go to school to learn how to create the good society, a world in which we can all live freely and responsibly to our greatest potential" (p. 5).

> *Learning needs emotion and challenge:* The proposers point out that the traditional supporting structures for children that once formed the rites of passage to adulthood are in disarray. Young people lack positive experience with adults within a community context and this loss of community brings with it problems that affect learning and life. "Our answer to these tendencies is the conviction that intellectual and social learning must be built upon a firm foundation of active experience in young people or, for that matter, in all people. Experience is not the end of education, but it is a means without which other goals are not attainable.

> "Exploring itself involves a willingness to draw and build upon one's knowledge and understanding and an openness to risk. Young people are quintessential explorers with their curiosity and freshness about what many adults have come to view as mundane. Young children generate questions and do not think in terms of compartmentalized learning. We intend to nurture and foster a

voyage of that spirit from childhood through adolescence and on to adulthood by using expeditionary learning" (p. 6).

Learning occurs with intimacy and caring: "Deeper relationships foster deeper and clearer thinking. Friendship best nourishes self-renewal both for adults and children. For this reason, our design proposes keeping teachers and students together for at least three years to create continuity and foster friendship for both. The antidote to insularity and alienation is not competition but friendship, the discovery of bonds and mutual commitment among human beings" (p. 7).

The collective and the individual can be brought together: "Kurt Hahn, who founded secondary schools in Germany and Scotland as well as Outward Bound, told students, 'You are crew not passengers.' When students are genuinely needed in a group, they respond with higher levels of commitment and performance. . . . Outward Bound has pioneered a pedagogy that addresses the severe motivational and self-esteem issues which prevent some students from learning how to learn as well as enhancing the growth of those who almost intuitively learn well. Outward Bound does this by putting all students on equal footing, with competition subordinated to cooperation, and with genuine opportunities for students at all levels of learning skill to test themselves and their deepest held values" (p. 7).

A fair assurance of success: Proposers are committed to a program devoted to improving human character and performance for all students. "This is accomplished through the sequential cycle of expeditionary learning where ambitious, yet realistic goals are set by participants. The teacher's role shifts from ensuring that students are adequately prepared to complete their challenge or problem with success to guaranteeing the safety of an expedition. Much as the Outward Bound instructor has safety paramount in his or her mind, teachers in our school will think and assist students in designing challenging intellectual, physical, and service expeditions where students' safety, intellectual and emotional, as well as their self-esteem are respected" (p. 8).

The having of wonderful ideas: "We view children neither as receptacles to be filled nor damaged goods to be patched. Instead, we are deeply respectful of the ideas children, adolescents and adults generate and the strengths and weaknesses they bring to every experience. Ideas are the sparks to start campfires which can light the darkness and warm us all. We view all children and teachers as scientists, inventors, writers, mathematicians, leaders, artists, linguists, and deeply compassionate human beings who are in the process of discovering and becoming. We want them to become more thoughtful, more knowledgeable, more confident and more courageous as they develop their minds, bodies and character to their fullest potential" (p. 8). Further, "We want to design schools that are homes to ideas, including the unexpected ideas of children and adults" (p. 9).

Solitude and reflection: "Every aspect of education must have times when children can be quiet, alone and reflective, not only to refresh their nervous systems, but to ask questions about themselves, to examine their inner lives, to discover for themselves their own springs of growth and self-renewal. Our schools—and hence our professional development as well—will help people to discover the talents they naturally possess, and show them how they might learn to work together, now and in the future, to use their talents more effectively. Those straining ever forward at the head of the pack have no greater privilege than to discover how to help shoulder the burden of stragglers, strangers to success" (p. 9).

Social vision: "Our stance is crystal clear on this point. To meet the challenge of school improvement, people must be able to visualize themselves as active learners in a common quest that will carry them together over the barriers that loom high in their lives. They must experience themselves unforgettably as members of a community worth defending against the negative influences they see everywhere around them and within them. . . . By viewing families and communities, as well as individual children, as possessing a reservoir of talents, strengths, passions and dreams our design engages entire communities in a process of development and in the realization of its aspirations through a change relationship to its schools" (pp. 10–11).

These are the design principles that will be used to help develop and organize schools for expeditionary learning. The curriculum will feature a sequence of interdisciplinary expeditions for students from prekindergarten through grade 12. The expeditions will interrelate the major academic disciplines, performance arts, and applied arts as well as physical development and service activities. Experiential learning, intellectual inquiry, reflection, service, and performance will characterize all the expeditions, whether they be short one-day affairs or longer journeys of several weeks.

To honor commitments to intimacy, continuity, spontaneity, and sustained effort over time, a fundamental unit of the school will be the "expedition watch" composed of eight to twelve students. These students will share responsibility for presenting research reports, solving problems, and otherwise working and playing together. Two to three watches will constitute a crew of approximately twenty-five students who, along with one expedition guide, will remain together for at least three years. When students are not on expedition, they will be in "base

camp" preparing for the next expedition. An expedition involving a fossil hunt in a nearby canyon, for example, requires a
good deal of advance preparation. The expedition provides an
"advanced organizer" for teaching geology, math, geography,
paleontology, zoology, and other subjects and for honing skills
in organizing and classifying data, writing, speaking, and so on.
Further, once the expedition is over students must return to base
camp to make sense of their journey, to organize their findings,
and to share their experience with others.

"This feature of going out and returning from learning
expeditions will demonstrate that for students to learn, there
must be a balance between learning how to learn, and acquiring
skills and the sharp slab of experience that challenges what one
has learned" (p. 15). To this end, "Students will complete several
major interdisciplinary expeditions each year, with the number
and duration varying. Students' portfolios will cumulatively reflect their work from their first expeditions. . . . At the beginning of every year a student will set goals in a videotaped
interview responding to the questions 'what do you want to learn
this year?' and 'what do you most love to do?' Every year the new
interview will be added to the same tape, creating a panoramic
and immediate view of child's aspirations and growth over as
many as fourteen years. These tapes will be enormously useful
for new teachers as they prepare to meet their new cycle of
students and tailor expeditions to individual students' needs. By
having all students participate, this·goalsetting becomes an
expeditionary learning ritual and important school tradition"
(pp. 18–19). Further, "To receive our diploma, our graduates will
successfully complete an individually designed and approved
senior service expedition as well as requirements and tests for
the International Baccalaureate degree. Students may begin to
meet prerequisite requirements for the senior service expedition beginning in the middle school years. Every expedition,
because it includes content area and assessment, serves as preparation for the requirements for the International Baccalaureate
degree" (p. 19).

Designing out from values can be scary for some teachers.
Many have never been asked what they think about such matters.

After all, visions are supposed to be something that administrators have but not teachers. Purposeful communities, however,
emerge from the individual visions of teachers and parents as
well as principals. Community building within the accelerated
schools movement points the way.

Henry M. Levin (Brandt, 1992) describes how he and his
colleagues work with teachers and principals interested in joining their "community of mind." Joining them means creating for
themselves a community of mind for their own school. "[We
asked them to] start by taking stock of their school in small
committees. They decide what dimensions of the school they
want to look at—but they have to look for strengths; that's very
important. . . everyone is involved including classified staff. . . .
We move from taking stock to developing a deep vision of the
future. This is not just a one-day inservice; it typically takes
weeks or months and involves reflection, deep thinking" (p. 23).
Levin invites them to "design as fully as possible the dream
school you would want for your own child or your grandchild, a
child very dear to you. . . . Our concern is whether they have a
vision in their *hearts* and a set of beliefs that drive their daily
behavior" (p. 23). Few teachers fail to respond to such an
invitation.

Community is part of our nature. Given the opportunity,
most of us will opt for community as the metaphor for how we
will live our lives and how we want our students to live their lives
in schools. We humans seek meaning and significance above all,
and building purposeful communities helps us to find both.

Using Curriculum
to Build Community

In this chapter we move to the next step: transforming purposes and shared values to decisions about what should be taught and how the curriculum should be organized. Purposeful communities are characterized by unified action. Members link what they do to shared values, conceptions, and ideas. Since members must work together, a plan for unified action is needed to help this transformation occur.

One way to formulate such a plan is to first develop an educational platform for the school. Once established, the platform provides a set of guidelines that principals and teachers can use to help make long-range and day-by-day decisions about their practice. The platform also represents a source of authority for justifying to ourselves and others what we are doing. Since this platform lets us and others know what we stand for, it helps answer the important "why" question.

What key elements should be included in a school's educational platform? To answer this question I rely on Robert J. Starratt's ideas drawn from our book, *Supervision: A Redefinition.* He believes that developing a platform brings about the kind of explicit intelligibility needed for principals and teachers to talk to each other and to others with greater clarity about what they do and why they do it. He proposes the following as general elements of an educational platform. Included are suggestions and ideas that can help schools decide for themselves what the elements will include.

1. *The aims of education.* Set down, in order of priority (if possible), the three most important aims of education—not simply education in the abstract, but education for the youngsters in your school system.

2. *Major achievements of students this year.* Bring these aims down to more specific application; identify the major achievements of students by the end of the year. (For example, mastery of some academic skills up to a certain level; the acquisition of certain basic principles that would govern behavior; more personal achievements, such as increased self-awareness or self-confidence, or trust and openness.)

3. *The social significance of the student's learning.* [Identify the extent emphasis should be given to] vocational learning; or the utilization of learning for good citizenship; or the acquisition of a particular cultural heritage.

4. *The image of the learner.* This element tries to uncover attitudes or assumptions about how one learns. Is the learner an empty vessel into which one pours information? Some may view the learner in a uniform way—as though all learners are basically the same and will respond equally to a uniform pedagogy. Some may use "faculty" psychology to explain how students learn. Some will focus on operant conditioning; others on targeting instruction to the cognitive developmental stages of concrete operations. Still others will differentiate among various styles and dispositions for learning that point to a greater emphasis on individualization of learning. [What value do we place on the various images? How can they be brought together to create a common image?]

5. *The image of the curriculum.* This element touches
upon attitudes about *what* the student learns. Some
say that the most important learnings are those
most immediately useful in "real" life. Others say
that any kind of learning is intrinsically valuable.
Others qualify the latter position and consider
some learnings, such as the humanities, to be intrinsically more valuable because they touch upon
more central areas of our culture. Others would
claim that the learning of subjects has value only
insofar as it categorizes people of different abilities
and interests and channels them in socially productive directions. Some might even claim that the
curriculum helps youngsters to understand God
better. [What value do we place on these various
images? How can they be brought together to create
a common image?]

6. *The image of the teacher.* What basically is a
teacher? Is a teacher an employee of the state, following the educational policies and practices dic-
tated by the local, state, and federal government?
Or is a teacher a professional specialist whom a
community employs to exercise his or her expertise
on behalf of youngsters? Or is a teacher a spokes-
person for tradition, passing on the riches of the
culture? Or is a teacher a political engineer, leading
youngsters to develop those skills necessary to reform their society? This element tries to elicit assumptions about the role of the teacher. [What
value do we place on these various images? How
can they be brought together to create a common
image?]

7. *The preferred pedagogy.* Will the teacher dominate the learning experience? Some assume that
inquiry learning is the best way to teach. Others
assume that each discipline lends itself better to
some forms of pedagogy than others. Some would

opt for a much more permissive, student-initiated learning enterprise. While there would understandably be some reluctance to focus on *one* pedagogical approach to the exclusion of all others, nonetheless, teachers tend to settle on two or three as the more effective approaches.

8. *The preferred school climate.* This element brings various environmental considerations into play, such as the affective tone to schoolwide and classroom discipline, feelings of student pride in the school, faculty morale, the openness of the school community to divergent lifestyles, expressive learnings, and individualistic ways of thinking and behaving. Some would describe an environment reflective of a learning community: open, caring, inquisitive, flexible, collaborative. Some would opt for order and predictability. Others would prefer a more relaxed climate, perhaps more boisterous but also more creative and spontaneous. This element is very much related to what is valued in the curriculum and to the social consequences of learning [Sergiovanni and Starratt, 1993, pp. 140–142].

Before these questions can be answered for a particular school, teachers will have to come to grips with their own platforms. And they will have to share their platforms with others. Sharing platforms is not easy but doing so helps teachers and principals become more reflective about their practice. The school's educational platform needs a high degree of polish. But individual teachers will probably want to tackle the job more informally. As Starratt explains, platform clarification "gives teachers names and words for telling their story. It enables them to talk with greater clarity among themselves, with parents, and with [colleagues]. . . about what they do. . . all platforms need not contain all of these elements; some may be expressed more in narrative form, some in a sequence of terse sentences; some may be expressed in pictures or cartoons" (p. 140). As teachers and principals work together to develop a platform for the school, a certain intrinsic logic begins to emerge. Assumptions about the nature of learning and preferred kinds of teacher-student relationships relate to aims. Aims relate to assumptions and assumptions to other elements. What the platform says about curriculum, therefore, influences and is influenced by all the other platform elements.

On the surface this discussion appears relativistic. As long as "everything hangs together," isn't one school's platform as good as another? In some respects the answer to this question is yes. Both the school effectiveness and the school-culture literatures, for example, suggest that focus and clarity are the key ingredients in the makeup of a successful school. The subject matter of this focus and clarity may well be secondary. These findings are sufficiently strong to assert that when accounting for the success of certain schools—"back to basics" Christian fundamentalist schools, Coalition of Essential Schools, Catholic parish schools, magnet public schools, ungraded elementary schools, or just plain-vanilla schools—the specifics of their undergirding educational philosophy may not be key. Philosophies among successful schools differ, often dramatically. Instead, success seems to be related to the fact that though substance differs, the schools have achieved focus and clarity and have embodied them in a unified practice.

Christ the King Elementary School in San Antonio, for example, has decided to make a commitment to a multicultural curriculum by adopting "Model for Cultural Understanding" as its metaphor for thinking about curriculum (Rodulfo, 1992). According to Father Janacek, pastor of Christ the King parish, "Everything we breathe is already Anglo culture. [The school] will provide possibilities outside that." Brother Peter Pontotillo, superintendent of Catholic schools for the San Antonio archdiocese, adds, "We want the children to be *biliteral*—fluent in both English and Spanish, and all the while make it possible for the student to identify who they are" (p. B-2).

Christ the King School plans to enroll 120 students, about 30 percent African American, 30 percent Anglo, and 40 percent Hispanic; the same percentages will hold for the faculty. The curriculum seeks to have all students learn to read and write well in both Spanish and English, and will emphasize cultural and religious experiences of all three groups. The aim is to have each student value his or her own culture while being sensitive to the cultures of others. University of Alaska sociologist Oscar Kawalgy (1992) believes that this kind of joined cultural emphasis on self and others can help students go beyond sympathy to empathy when viewing other cultures. When this happens they develop a sense of pride without arrogance in their own culture. While Christ the King students will be expected to meet rigorous academic standards, success will be evaluated as well by attitudinal surveys that address cultural issues.

Just a few miles across town the Hawthorne Elementary School is moving full speed ahead in implementing the core knowledge curriculum, as espoused by E. D. Hirsch in his book *Cultural Literacy: What Every American Needs to Know* (1987) and spelled out in a series of other books themed to what every child should know for a particular grade level. The Hirsch curriculum specifies about half of the content to be covered. Hawthorne plans to use the remaining half to emphasize multicultural parallels to the largely Eurocentric prescribed curriculum. Even allowing for this multicultural emphasis, the Hawthorne approach differs dramatically from the Christ the King approach. Yet both schools are intent on creating inclusive learning communities and both show promises of success. The key, in each case, appears to be the potential for unified action that is achieved by focus and clarity.

Jerry Litt, principal of the Mohegan School in New York City's District 12, puts it this way: "Ultimately everyone in the school must have a common sense of purpose. Teachers must have some real responsibility, some stake in the school. Parents must have some leverage to hold schools accountable. If you have these elements in place, any school—whether its focus is circus arts or computer technology—works beautifully" (Center for Educational Innovation, 1992, p. 8).

Are focus and clarity enough, however, to qualify a school as a community? The answer has to be *yes* if the school's underlying theory is on the *gemeinschaft* side of the ledger and *no* if the school's underlying theory is on the *gesellschaft* side. It is the nature of relationships among students, between students and teachers, and between teachers and administrators that will determine whether community exists and not just the prevailing educational philosophy or the chosen curriculum. To become a community, in other words, the school's community of mind must include not only the valued curriculum approach but the valued character of relationships for the school. Certain curriculum choices, however, are more likely to foster relationships that contribute to community building than others.

As we saw in Chapter Two, *gemeinschaft* relationships are characterized by adults being personally involved in the lives of the students they serve. Students are not clients, customers, or cases, but objects of stewardship. Stewardship requires that adults have a personal stake in the academic success and the social welfare of each student. Stewardship requires that adults bring a collective orientation rather than self-orientation to bear in their relationships to students and with each other, placing the common good over their own particular interests. If a collective orientation means being a generalist rather than a specialist, a counselor and friend as well as a teacher, and a problem solver rather than a problem sender, then so be it. Stewardship requires an orientation toward specifics rather than universals. Decisions must be made in use, as on-the-spot evaluations of the specifics of a given situation dictate. The standard explication of universal codes and rules, regardless of circumstances, is, therefore, a rare occasion. Finally, stewardship requires that love and belonging not be conditional. Students are held to high expectations and achievement is valued, but one's acceptance as a valued person is not connected to what one achieves.

In *gemeinschaft*, means are not only ways to achieve ends but are ends in themselves. Mastering the curriculum is not only a means to graduate but is valued in its own right. The Federalist papers, for example, are celebrations of democracy and models of civil discourse. Knowledge about them is good, period. Loving students not only helps them learn but is a good thing to do. We should love students even if learning were not affected.

In community, shared conceptions about curriculum are essential to developing a community of mind among teachers and between them and others. And shared conceptions are necessary to develop a practice of teaching that resembles unified action. At the same time, personalized learning, a commitment to professional community, and the realities involved in teaching different students, different things, in different situations require that teachers be given considerable freedom in their practice. Thus, both *discipline* and *discretion* are needed to make community work.

One way to achieve balance between discipline and discretion is to provide guidelines that schools and individual teachers can use to evaluate whether the curriculum decisions they make are consistent with shared values. Guidelines may take the form of principles, standards, assumptions about learning, and general outcomes. Good guidelines need to be firm enough and directional enough to shape school and individual teacher decisions without determining what those decisions will be. Different objectives, different situations, different teachers, different students, and different needs all lead to different decisions. Though different in these ways, the decisions will be the same for having embodied the same guidelines.

The approach to curriculum development in Ontario provides a model for achieving balance between discipline and discretion. (See Brown, 1991, for a detailed overview of the Ontario plan.) The Canadian model can help both states and school districts in the United States come to grips with the balance issue. The Ontario Ministry of Education established a common framework of goals and aims that describes the learning opportunities school programs throughout the province should make available to students. By doing so, the ministry sought to provide a general direction, complete with compass settings, without getting involved in mapmaking or in charting travel routes. Schools, of course, remain accountable to the ministry. But instead of following a provincial script, they are required to demonstrate that their curriculum, teaching, and evaluation decisions embody the provincial framework.

The ministry's position is that the major responsibility for planning curriculum should rest with the school; this is the only way schools can respond to the special needs and characteristics of the children in their care. Further, "much of the necessary planning (and in some situations almost all of it, especially in relation to day-to-day activities) must be done by the individual teacher. Certain important parts of the planning process are, however, best done, co-operatively, in some cases by the entire teaching staff, and in some cases by all the teachers of a given division. Individual teachers have the responsibility of selecting strategies, resources, and activities appropriate to the needs of individual children who should then be involved in setting short-term objectives, in devising ways and means of accomplishing tasks, and in choosing activities" (Ontario Ministry of Education, 1975b).

To help the process along, the ministry provides the following suggestions:

> When framing objectives for specific learning experiences, the teacher may find the following questions helpful:
>
> - Do these objectives interpret and support the major provisional goals?
> - Which are the most important objectives?
> - Are these objectives consistent with one another?
> - Are these objectives realistic and appropriate for the child or children concerned?
> - What are the conditions under which learning is to take place?
> - What assumptions about learning must be considered in selecting teaching approaches for these objectives?
> - What are the criteria for the assessment of achievement? [Ontario Ministry of Education, 1975a, p. 8].

The ministry is not afraid to state its values and to make its intentions clear. In *Education in the Primary and Junior Divisions*

(Ontario Ministry of Education, 1975a), it notes that though teachers should be guided primarily by their own knowledge of students, they should nonetheless be informed by the findings of current research. The document then describes two major emphases found in the literature: behaviorist theory and cognitive development theory. Acknowledging that the behaviorist approach has a role to play, it nonetheless asserts that "of the two approaches, cognitive explanation is more appropriate in dealing with complex behaviours such as communication, concept-formation, and problem solving" (p. 10).

With respect to individual differences, *Education in the Primary and Junior Divisions* states that "implicit in the philosophy of this document is the idea of acceptance — the acceptance by the school of all children with their wide variations in ability, physique and personality" (p. 10). The document also comments on the importance of being sensitive to the special needs of children and insists that whatever decisions teachers make they must reflect concern for concept development across the curriculum.

The ministry avows its belief that certain assumptions about children and learning are basic to the curriculum framework provided, and that these assumptions will be embodied in the decisions that teachers and schools make. The assumptions are:

- Children are curious. Their need to explore and manipulate should be fulfilled through handling real things that involve more than one sense. The more all the senses are involved, the more effective the experience.
- Most human activity is a purposeful search for pattern. This includes organizing new information and relating it to previously developed concepts. Incongruity between old patterns and new experiences stimulates questioning, observation, manipulation, and application in a variety of new situations. Maintaining the right balance between novel and familiar experiences in learning situations is one of the most vital tasks in the art of teaching.

- Learning experiences gain power if they are part of organized and meaningful wholes.
- Children have an intrinsic need for mastery over situations,
  a need that they express by using their experiences to search
  out the significant patterns in reality and thus reduce
  uncertainty.
- Children find self-fulfillment in successful learning, and are
  not motivated merely by external rewards and approval.
  Pupils engaged in self-rewarding activity with a sensitive,
  consistent teacher who makes demands appropriate to their
  own level are having a happy experience.
- Play is an essential part of learning. It is free from the
  restrictions of reality, external evaluations, and judgment.
  Children can try out different styles of action and communication without being required to make premature decisions or being penalized for errors. Play provides a context
  in which the teacher can observe children's handling of
  materials and social situations, assess their stage of development, and encourage experiences that further their growth.
  The teacher should know when to intervene unobtrusively,
  when to add to or change a play situation, when to provide a
  toy telephone, a costume, a question, or a suggestion that
  will further the fantasy or broaden the experience.
- Children learn through experience with people, symbols,
  and things. Things may be objects, events, processes, or
  relationships.
- The symbolic process for children develops through a sequence of representation. Initially children must understand that a real object can be represented by such symbols
  as a spoken word, gesture, dramatic movement, toy, model,
  picture; ultimately they must understand that an object can
  be represented by the printed word. The development of
  symbolism underlies the communication, recording, and
  coding of experience in a condensed and systematic form.
  Full understanding of symbols, however, is slow to emerge
  (Ontario Ministry of Education, 1975a, pp. 15–16).

The ministry believes that content is more than subject
matter contained in a textbook. It includes information, values,

concepts, techniques, strategies, and skills. This content is embedded in an environment made up of people, things, and symbols. The ministry does not, however, specify the content that must be followed. Instead, *Education in the Primary and Junior Divisions* provides standards for selecting content:

> Both the teacher and child should be involved in choosing content. If the teacher starts the process, he or she must pose a question or initiate an activity that catches the imagination of the child. If children are encouraged to pursue topics of individual interest, there are likely to be as many questions as there are children. The children's involvement is important because content that they have chosen themselves is most likely to motivate learning [p. 17].

> In either case, the teacher fashions the topic into a content vehicle through which he or she can assess the needs of each child and through which the child is enabled to acquire the values, concepts, information, opinions, techniques, learning strategies, and skills that the teacher has identified as the objectives of the curriculum. The teacher should not, however, ignore opportunities for learning that arise outside the context of planned objectives [pp. 17–18].

Having clearly stated that content decisions should be consistent with the general goals of education provided, with the assumptions about children and how they learn, and with other elements of the provisional framework, the document then provides a set of criteria that teachers can use in selecting content:

- Will it give children an opportunity for direct inquiry, independent study, and creative ability in the context of their own interests, abilities, and developmental needs? Will it fulfill their needs to explore and to manipulate? Will it capitalize on the use of all their senses?

- Will it satisfy the children's search for pattern
  by building concepts that can be developed
  and related to other learning?
- Will it relate to what the children already know?
- Will it be sufficiently novel to stimulate questions, observations, and manipulations?
- Will the children be able to see what they are
  learning as part of an organized and meaningful whole?
- Will it spring from real experiences in the children's environment? Is it relevant to their understanding of the world? Is this content appropriate to each child's level of development?
- With this content as a vehicle, will the children
  be able to know when they have been successful? Will it fulfill the children's basic needs
  for mastery? Will it provoke questions, involvement, and a desire for further exploration?
- Will it utilize all the channels of learning—
  visual, auditory, motor-manipulative, olfactory,
  gustatory, and tactile?
- Will it encourage learning through play?
- Will it provide experiences with qualitative relationships such as texture, colour, and sounds,
  and with quantitative relationships such as
  number, distance, size, and mass?
- Will this content provide opportunities for various techniques of investigation?
- Will this knowledge or technique be personally
  or socially useful? Will it help children to learn
  skills that will help them to manipulate, observe, reason, record, and communicate?
- Will this content lead to a reasoned knowledge
  of and pride in Canada and motivate children
  to build their own understanding of their environment and community? [p. 18].

The document then addresses a series of related issues including
the role of skills, how time should be used, grouping practices, the

use of space, and so on. It provides examples on how the framework might be (but not must be) implemented across the curriculum. Throughout, the emphasis is on students learning to use
their minds well, on personalized teaching, and on active learning. A similar framework is provided for schools in the intermediate and senior divisions (Ontario Ministry of Education, 1989).

Key to the Ontario experience is providing enough of a
sense of direction to help create communities of mind and
unified practices without compromising the discretion needed
to nurture the school as a professional community, caring community, learning community, and inquiring community. The
guidelines help shape a given school's educational platform.
Together, the guidelines and the platform help teachers to answer such questions as: What are we doing? How are we doing it?
What is involved in doing it? Why are we doing it? What are its
basic assumptions? Is what we are doing consistent with what we
believe? What is the quality of the experience it affords students?
Do we still want to do this? If yes, can we do it better? If not, what
alternatives are there?

Another way in which discipline and discretion can be
achieved is by striking a balance among instructional, problem-
solving, and expressive outcomes as curriculum experiences are
planned (Eisner, 1969, 1979). Instructional outcomes are set
beforehand and in fairly specific ways. They are stated in terms
of what the student is supposed to be able to do as a result of
teaching. Curriculum and teaching decisions are made by designing down from the instructional outcomes. Problem-solving
outcomes are shaped by the decisions made about problems
that students must solve and exhibitions they must master and
perform. Expressive outcomes are discovered during and after
the teaching of trusted subject matter and the use of trusted
teaching activities ("trusted" means that they are known for their
ability to stimulate learning).

In a sense, instructional outcomes represent baseball
strike zones. And teaching to them represents pitching learning
into a particular strike zone. Balls and strikes must be called to
keep track of how effective the teaching is in achieving the
outcomes. For example, in teaching a lesson or unit on the jury
system we might state the following instructional outcomes:

(a) the student will be able to differentiate between the roles and functions of various principals in a jury trial (prosecuting attorney, defense attorney, bailiff, types of witnesses); (b) the student will be able to write two coherent paragraphs that describe the differences in rules of evidence for civil trials as opposed to criminal trials. If the student performs according to the specified behaviors, then we have a strike. If not, then it's a ball and that pitch doesn't count, even though what the student learns may be more important than the stated instructional outcome. The student, for example, may not be able to explain the rules of evidence as required but is able to detect flaws in arguments better than before. The student may not be able to differentiate the various roles very well but has a greater appreciation for the fairness and effectiveness of the judicial system. Sorry, it's still a ball. The learning doesn't count because it does not fit into the strike zone.

In the real world of teaching, good teachers often change their minds as they teach. Sometimes they chase a student's ideas and wind up at a place different than originally intended. The strike zone that counts for them moves to another position. But the strike zone that counts officially stands still, converting perfectly sound and sensible strikes into balls.

When using only instructional outcomes, the curriculum intended, the curriculum taught, and the curriculum learned must always be aligned with each other. Thus once outcomes are set (discipline), teachers have increasingly less say over the taught and learned curriculum (discretion). It often makes sense to insist that students be able to demonstrate exactly what they are supposed to. Thus, instructional outcomes have an important role to play. But so do problem-solving and expressive outcomes. Balance is needed among the three if both discipline and discretion are to be achieved.

Problem-solving outcomes are harder to nail down in a specific way beforehand. But they are hardly serendipitous. By carefully crafting a problem, we can increase the likelihood that certain kinds of outcomes will emerge. As Eisner (1979) explains, "The problem-solving objective differs in a significant way from the behavioral [instructional] objective. In the problem-solving objective, the students formulate or are given a problem to solve—say to find out how deterrents to smoking might be made more effective, or how to design a paper structure that will hold two bricks sixteen inches above a table, or how the variety and quality of food served in the school cafeteria could be increased within the existing budget" (p. 101). It's not enough just to state the problem; certain criteria need to be provided that set a standard for how the problem will be solved. The more specific the criteria, the more the range of outcomes becomes narrowed. The forms of the solution, however, remain infinite. With instructional outcomes both questions and answers are set beforehand. With problem-solving outcomes, the question is set but the answer is not definite.

Problems-based learning provides a happy balance between discipline and discretion for both teachers and students. Teachers might agree, for example, on the problems that students will solve in a given unit, course, or grade level. But since no single answer or no one solution exists for the typical problem, teachers have flexibility in making choices about what will be studied, what materials will be used, what teaching approaches to use, what learning settings to invent, and so on. Students have discretion too. Within the parameters of the problem, they decide how they will learn and what they will learn. As teachers monitor learning, they make decisions that shape what students are doing and they make decisions that are shaped by what students are doing. Despite discretion, a certain coherence and focus are maintained by the parameters the problem provides.

Problem-solving outcomes play a major role in organizing the curriculum, arranging learning experiences, teaching, and evaluating in schools that are committed to the principles of the Coalition of Essential Schools. These schools rely heavily on exhibitions of mastery as the construct for organizing the curriculum, for teaching and learning, and for evaluating. Ted Sizer, in his book *Horace's School* (1992), provides some examples of problems:

1. Select one of the following familiar human emotions: fear, envy, courage, hunger, longing, joy, anger, greed, jealousy.

In an essay, define the emotion you choose, drawing on your own and others' experience. Then render a similar definition using in turn at least three of the following forms of expression: a written language other than English; a piece of drawing, painting, or sculpture; photographs, a video, or film; a musical composition; a short story or play; pantomime; a dance.

Select examples from literature, journalism, the arts, and history of other people's definitions or representations of the emotion you have chosen. These should strike you as important and arresting, even if they do not correspond with your own definition.

Be ready in four months to present this work and to answer questions about it. The Exhibition— a portfolio collected by you over the next months— will be judged on the basis of its vitality and overall coherence as well as the quality of its individual components [p. 23].

2.   Your group of five classmates is to complete accurately the federal Internal Revenue Service Form 1040 for each of five families. Each member of your group will prepare the 1040 for one of the families. You may work in concert, helping one another. "Your" particular family's form must be completed by you personally, however.

Attached are complete financial records for the family assigned to you, including the return filed by that family last year. In addition, you will find a blank copy of the current 1040, including related schedules, and explanatory material provided by the Internal Revenue Service.

You will have a month to complete this work. Your result will be "audited" by an outside expert and one of your classmates after you turn it in. You will have to explain the financial situation of "your" family and to defend the 1040 return for it which you have presented.

Each of you will serve as a "co-auditor" on the return filed by a student from another group. You will be asked to comment on that return.

Good luck. Getting your tax amount wrong— or the tax for any of the five families in your group—could end you in legal soup! [p. 48].

Sizer notes that a problem themed to Form 1040 is likely to appeal to students since it represents an unavoidable dimension of real life. It deals with two important issues with which they must be concerned throughout their lives: money and fairness. He explains, "Taught intelligently, it opens the door wide, and for many students in a compelling way to a cluster of important disciplines such as microeconomics, politics, ethics, and political history. It can thereby be the springboard for sustained serious study in several directions" (p. 49). This problem, in other words, allows for the designing out of numerous decisions about curriculum, teaching, and learning, as well as about evaluation.

In Chapter Five, the expeditionary learning model was discussed as an example of how one designs out from values. This model too relies heavily on problem-solving outcomes. This problem from expeditionary learning provides more detail than previous examples but still allows teachers and students leeway.

Sample expedition: mapping and navigation expedition

Principal theme: Scale and structure

The study of scale and structure of Earth, landforms, the solar system, and beyond allows students to develop an appreciation of their relationship to their geographic surroundings. It also extends their frontiers beyond their immediate surroundings.

Principal objective: Develop an ability to describe movement from one location to another in a com-

munity, on Earth, in the Solar System, in the Galaxy
and in the Universe.

Activity objectives: Upon completion of a series of
activities in the expedition, a student will be
able to:

- Trace the development of our knowledge of mapping and navigation.
- Compare and contrast ancient and modern methods for determining geographic and magnetic direction.
- Construct models of ancient astronomical instruments and observatories.
- Compare and contrast ancient and modern maps of Earth.
- Measure Earth's circumference.
- Determine exact location on Earth's surface.
- Construct and interpret topographic maps of specific geographic areas.
- Use instruments to measure location, distance and time.
- Compute values for direction, distance, time and speed.
- Construct a true scale model of the solar system.
- Predict the position of the planets in the night sky.
- Plan an interplanetary expedition.
- Compare the size of the solar system with the Milky Way galaxy and the entire universe.
- Apply the concept of scale to the design of a structure.
- Design an orienteering course for the community.
- Assist community agencies in the planning and preservation of parks, gardens, building sites, etc. ["Expeditionary Learning," 1992, p. 35].

Expressive outcomes, according to Eisner (1969), are what one ends up with, whether intended or not, after being engaged in a learning experience. "Expressive outcomes are the consequences of curriculum activities that are intentionally planned to provide a fertile ground for personal purposing and experiences" (p. 26). The emphasis is on the activity itself, the learning experience that the student will be engaged in, the content or the subject matter, and not the specifics of what the student will learn as a result of this engagement.

Expressive outcomes, while unanticipated, are nonetheless valued learnings. Over the years, good teachers come to know and trust the potential of certain ideas, certain activities, and certain learning experiences to promote learning. They know that when students engage in them, good things happen. The accomplished kindergarten teacher, for example, has confidence that when kids and sandboxes are mixed, learning takes place. Add a little water and the learning multiplies. But it's hard to predict just what it is that the student will learn. An English teacher knows that teaching *Gatsby* works. If done properly, kids get a lot out of it. While the teacher may have in mind certain kinds of outcomes, she or he remains open, indeed receptive, to the magic of *Gatsby* to elicit other kinds of outcomes from students. Holding a week-long jury trial is a tried-and-true learning activity. It takes a lot of planning to set up the right scenario, to provide roles and descriptions for everyone, and to make sure that the trial unfolds without a hitch. But it's worth the effort. Though the teacher can't say exactly what students will get out of it, she or he has always found that they learn a great deal when engaged in this particular exercise.

Again, we return to Eisner. "Yet surely there must be room in school for activities that promise to be fruitful, even though the teacher might not be able to say what specifically the students will learn or experience. Parents do this all the time. The trip to the zoo, weekends spent camping in the woods, the bicycle ride after dinner; no specific objective or problems are posed prior to setting out on such activities, yet we feel that they will be enjoyable and that some 'good' will come from them" (1979, p. 104).

Instructional outcomes, problem-solving outcomes, and expressive outcomes all have important roles to play in curriculum planning. When brought together, they allow teachers to make decisions that reflect the discipline necessary for purposeful community building. Further, this discipline is achieved without compromising the discretion needed to make informed decisions in light of the ambiguities found in the typical teaching and learning situation. Discretion increases the likelihood that effective teaching and learning decisions will be made and that effective caring decisions will be made. Discretion allows the building of an inquiring community as teachers puzzle together over what decisions make the most sense. And discretion embodies the professional community by allowing teachers to take control of their practice.

7

The Classroom as Democratic Community

On the first day of school, new first-grade teacher Patricia Cullen asked her thirty six-year-old students to be quiet seventy-seven times. The first day went like this:

7:30 A.M.: Mrs. Cullen arrives at school an hour early to review her lesson plan.

8:29 A.M.: She heads downstairs to the schoolyard to collect new students and begins her first attempt at line-forming. The children bump each other with their heads and tummies. Then, standing in a zig-zag, they meander to their classroom. More than half the parents come into the room as well. One child starts to cry. A mother calls her son over and pours asthma medicine into his mouth. He runs back to his seat holding a plastic toy troll with hot pink hair.

9:07 A.M.: Two more children show up. Most parents leave, though two linger in the hallway, waving. Mrs. Cullen begins a group activity, a song called, "Hey, Hey, Look at Me." Each child takes a turn at two lines of the song. The group loses interest after the 20th child's turn and starts to talk.

9:32 A.M.: A teacher walks in and hands Mrs. Cullen a folder. Children start poking one another. One

117

child asks to go to the bathroom. Six others try to follow.

9:50 A.M.: A reading teacher appears for a short lesson. Trying to get the attention of a child with "Ricky" on his nametag, the teacher calls him "Richard" four times. When "Ricky" doesn't respond, another child explains his name is Enrique.

10 A.M.: The principal delivers a student-teacher to Mrs. Cullen, who says she is not prepared to help another teacher learn. She asks that the student-teacher be reassigned.

12:10 P.M.: Children return to the room after lunch and put their heads on their tables for rest time.

12:11 P.M.: Students raise their heads and begin talking. Mrs. Cullen gives up on rest time and starts collecting their notebooks.

12:26 P.M.: Mrs. Cullen turns the lights off, as a warning to them to be quiet. It works. "Isn't that beautiful?" she says, smiling with relief as she turns the light back on. During the next hour, she flips the lights three more times. By the fourth flip, the class ignores her. One girl makes her third trek to the bathroom. Another girl, saying she is going to vomit, asks to go, too. Mrs. Cullen moves to assist Letika, who has hit her head on the windowsill.

1 P.M.: The first graders draw self-portraits with crayons. Some color carefully. Others scribble. One rips his into pieces and throws it away. Another turns his into a paper airplane and flies it across the room.

1:30 P.M.: Mrs. Cullen orders a boy out of his hiding place in a coat closet.

1:35 P.M.: Another reading teacher, a veteran, appears unexpectedly and helps quiet the class while Mrs. Cullen gives instructions.

2:40 P.M.: The first graders are told to assemble in two lines at the door. They form a clump instead and insist on visiting the bathroom.

2:55 P.M.: Dismissal time. The children bounce past Mrs. Cullen into the schoolyard. "I'm mentally spent," she says to another new teacher, Laura Schwartz, as she tidies her classroom. "I had a rotten day" [Tabor, 1992, p. 58].

Mrs. Cullen's second day went a little bit better. She told the principal she didn't want any interruptions, managed to separate students who were particularly troublesome, and gave slower and clearer instructions to the children. And the boy who tore up his self-portrait had drawn a new one. Mrs. Cullen

made one of the more disruptive boys a line leader, holding his hand often. "I realized he just needed some extra attention," she said. The children managed their first writing exercise. They earned their snack. And when she called them to do their final line-up for the day, they moved quickly. "I mean quiet and I'm serious," she reminded them, her voice hoarse, but confident.

With their backpacks on, her 30 mostly quiet minions trooped through the halls, clumping up only a few times. As they scattered to join parents and friends, Mrs. Cullen stopped to speak to several mothers, one of whom asked how her son had done. "He was great," the teacher said, smiling at the boy. "Much better. Right?" He grinned, then ducked his head bashfully. "Right," he replied [Tabor, 1992, p. 58].

Getting and maintaining control in the classroom is important. But *how* one gets and maintains this control makes an important difference in what students learn and in the quality of classroom life that teachers and students share. Some approaches to discipline emphasize student compliance with the teacher's commands and rules. The prime purpose is to modify the students' behavior. Teachers are encouraged to assert themselves by taking control of the classroom. Other approaches emphasize students accepting responsibility for their own behavior. The prime purpose is to delineate consequences for "good" and "bad" behavior and then teach students to accept responsibility for the choices they make. And still other approaches are themed to helping classrooms become democratic communities. The purpose of these approaches is to teach students citizenship and to help them become caring adults.

In the beginning, new teachers like Patricia Cullen aren't fussy about the approach they use. They are interested in finding something that works. They want to get enough order in the classroom so that students will listen to them and to each other. But there is a difference between the overall strategy that one adopts and the tactics one might use at any given moment. There is a difference between getting enough order in the classroom to begin with and working on a long-term approach to classroom life. During the first two days, Mrs. Cullen didn't hesitate to use rewards and consequences now and then to get compliance. But her overall aim was to show the children she cared for them and to encourage them to care for each other.

In communities the best discipline strategies are those that teach students citizenship and help students become caring adults. The aim is for the classroom (and the school itself) to become a democratic community. Democratic communities have rules and use rewards and consequences, albeit sparingly. These are not at the heart of what matters. Key are the standards, values, and commitments that make up a constitution for living together. In democratic communities norms count more than rules. And control is embedded in the community's norm structure. Members of the community are motivated to behave in certain ways because of the obligations they feel to abide by these norms.

Democratic community is aimed not just at improving student behavior but at creating the kinds of ties that bond students together and students and teachers together and that bind them to shared ideas and ideals. When students share the responsibility for developing norms and when their commitment to these norms is expected, they know they belong. They get the message that they are needed. They feel a sense of ownership in the classroom. They experience community. These ties are the antidote to the loss of community that many students are experiencing in their everyday lives.

To be alienated, wrote Urie Bronfenbrenner (1986) "is to lack a sense of belonging, to feel cut off from family, friends, school or work—the four worlds of childhood" (p. 430). It is getting more and more difficult for students to experience the four worlds of childhood. Families are struggling harder and need more help. The *gesellschaft* characteristics of schools make it difficult for them to pick up the slack, to provide what families are unable to provide. Increasingly young people are stuck with each other, forced to rely more on each other to meet their own needs.

Cusick (1992), for example, argues that *gesellschaft* schools are structured and function in ways that actually drive students away from their studies and back into their own groups. Student subcultures become stronger and more distant as a result. In his words,

> The bureaucracy absorbs students' time, not their energy, and for students in the midst of the differentiated and dense routine, there is a great deal of waiting around with little to do. Schools mass their people just as do armies, stadiums, and prisons, where people spend a lot of time waiting around for others to do something or watching others do something. In schools, the other is a teacher who, in the interest of articulating the school's limited notion of what is appropriate, initiates the activity and maintains the center of the interaction. Of the mass of students, schools demand attendance, passive compliance, and limited attention but not a lot more. Adding up the time spent on announcements or receiving assignments, coming and going,

eating, waiting, and watching, and otherwise com-
plying with the procedural demands, students experience a great deal of empty space in the day
[p. 32].

Cusick points out that left to themselves, students turn to each
other and not to their studies. "Friends offer intensity and exhilaration that fill the empty spaces and offset the bureaucratic
tedium. . . . Students slide easily from class to group activity. To
offset that tendency, teachers de-emphasize cooperative projects
and encourage instead each student to attend to his or her own
learning. In effect there is a reciprocal and dynamic relationship between the students' tendency to group and the
school's group approach to instruction" (p. 32).

Student subcultures have always given students their own
separate identity. But what was once a mere rift between that
subculture and the official school culture is turning into a
chasm. In too many cases adults are not significantly part of
students' lives. This distancing not only makes our work difficult but places students at risk socially and behaviorally.
Compliance-oriented and even responsibility-oriented student
discipline strategies are not able to heal this rift. Compliance
strategies actually make things worse. Responsibility strategies
are helpful but just not powerful enough. Strategies aimed at
helping classrooms become democratic communities, on the
other hand, can help young people reconnect with each other
and with their schoolwork. Democratic communities can help
students and adults come together to construct a standard for
living their school lives together. And democratic communities
can help students meet their needs to belong, to be active, to
have control, and to experience sense and meaning in their
lives.

References to democracy in schools sometimes raises anxiety levels. Images of freedom gone awry, even anarchy, quickly
dance into our minds. "We can't let teachers, and especially
students, do whatever they please." "You just can't run a school by
voting." "Kids have too much freedom as it is." Most of us would

agree with these observations. The problem is that they reflect a vernacular view of freedom that misses the point.

The Constitution, the U.S. Bill of Rights, and the Canadian Charter of Rights and Freedoms, for example, are unflinching testimonies to democratic values that define the obligations of citizenship. As cornerstones of our society, they are the bedrock values that define our nations as democratic communities. Thus it is a paradox to find ambivalence when someone suggests that these same values be applied close to home. At the heart of any democratic community is active citizenship. The price of active citizenship is measured in obligations, duties, and commitment to the common good. Yes, the subject matter of democracy includes individual freedoms but these freedoms can be guaranteed only by the strength of active citizenship. The Bill of Rights, for example, should more accurately be thought of as "The Bill of Obligations." Without a commitment in both our personal and public lives to ensure that these rights are lived, without a commitment to accept the obligations of active citizenship, any litany of rights becomes a litany of empty platitudes.

Schools and classrooms as democratic communities embrace adults as well as students. Active citizenship forces everyone to get into each other's pockets by requiring them to come to grips with a collective image of school life, to work together to solve problems, to invest together in the welfare of the community, and to live together in accordance with community norms. In a democratic community, the official culture is not imposed by one on another but is created together. Democratic communities make demands on all of their members. Teachers, administrators, and students all have obligations and duties to each other and to the school that must be met. These demands let members know that they are needed by the community and belong to the community, thus further solidifying the ties that bind and bond.

Adults, of course, have special roles to play in developing and living democratic community in schools. It is their responsibility to ensure that relationships with each other and with students model the best that active citizenship has to offer. It is

their responsibility to teach students the values of democracy
and the skills of active citizenship. It is their responsibility to
show students how these values and skills can lead to the development of standards and codes for living together. It is their
responsibility to teach students the obligations of citizenship to
the common good. And it is their responsibility to teach the
importance of community members caring for each other.

Democratic communities help students to *be* as well as to
become. They seek to help students meet their needs today as well
as become tomorrow's caring and active citizens. Unless today's
needs are met, students drift further away from school life. The
more *gesellschaft* is the school and the more *gesellschaft* its approach to discipline, the less likely will students' needs be met
and the more likely will students drift away.

Gesellschaft discipline strategies, for example, are based on
bureaucratic theories and on certain psychological theories that
are designed to "manage" behavior. Bureaucratic theories encourage reliance on explicit policies and numerous universal
rules aligned with explicit procedures. And these psychological
theories encourage reliance on extrinsic rewards and punishments linked to rules as behavioral-consequence contingencies.
Like training pigeons, teachers use rewards and punishments to
get students to behave. Few lessons are taught. Few reasons are
given. Few appeals are made to moral questions and issues. And
little attention is given to meeting students' needs.

Gemeinschaft strategies, by contrast, are designed to teach,
to encourage students to respond for intrinsic and moral reasons, to let students know that they are cared for and that they
must learn to care for others. Emphasis is given to shared
standards, customs, mores, agreements, values, and commitments. Instead of striking behavioral contracts, the emphasis is
on teachers and students together developing a social and moral
constitution that spells out what is right and good for the community, what each member of the community can expect from
others, and what each member must give in return. As a school
moves away from the *gesellschaft* end of the continuum toward
gemeinschaft, do's and don'ts that manage behavior are ex-
changed for rights and wrongs that teach lessons about caring,

citizenship, and community. With a social and moral constitution in place, teachers can respond to discipline problems as follows:

The Event	What is happening? What is the student doing that is causing a problem?
The Social Contract	What are our agreements? What are our commitments to each other, to the class, to the school?
The Moral Connection	Why is what is happening wrong? How has the standard fallen?
Next Steps	What must be done to fix things up? What natural consequences will be endured? For grave infractions, what rational consequences must be endured?
Revisiting Commitments	Looking ahead, what are our commitments to each other and to this community?

In such an environment, let us watch discipline in action. Consider Chris. Her homework assignment was to stop off at the library on the way home to "look up some stuff" her group needed to complete a project. But when she came to school the next day, she hadn't completed the assignment. The teacher asked why. If something important prevented Chris from completing the assignment she would have been excused, but she simply "forgot." The teacher reminded her about what it means to meet one's commitments to classmates and to the class itself. Together teacher and Chris discuss how important it is to be dependable and what happens when someone does not carry his or her own load. Chris reflects on how she would feel if the leader or another student let her down. Chris agrees to get the assignment done tonight and offers to gather some additional information as well. The group is disturbed with Chris and lets her know how they feel. The group, for example, will now be late getting the project finished and that means messing up the reporting schedule. No one in the class is happy about that. (If Chris was involved in a grave infraction—fighting, for example—not only would she endure natural consequences but rational consequences as well. She might, for example, be required to stay after school or even face suspension.) Finally, Chris is asked to renew her commitment to the classroom constitution.

Shifting from *gesellschaft* rules to *gemeinschaft* standards means relying less on bureaucratic and psychological manipulation and more on moral authority. The *gemeinschaft* approach is the natural way that groups characterized by caring handle things. Healthy families, for example, are more inclined to handle problems in this manner. Family actions are teaching actions and family lessons are lessons in values.

Healthy families are also naturally positioned to provide for the needs of members. In *Reclaiming Youth at Risk* Larry Brendtro, Martin Brokenleg, and Steve Van Bockern (1990) provide a compelling argument for schools to rely on traditional Native American child-rearing philosophies as the metaphor to guide community-building efforts and development of compatible discipline strategies:

1. Recognition of the universal need to *belong*
2. Guaranteeing opportunities for *mastery*
3. Encouraging the expression of *independence*
4. Teaching the value of *generosity*

Brendtro and colleagues point out that self-esteem is widely recognized as a primary goal in socializing children. Without a sense of self-worth children in any culture are likely to experience a number of social, psychological, and learning problems. They cite the definitive work of Stanley Coopersmith (1967) in identifying four basic components of self-esteem:

1. *Significance.* Significance is found in the acceptance, attention and affection of others. To lack significance is to be rejected, ignored and not to belong.
2. *Competence* develops as one masters the environment. Suc-

cess brings innate satisfaction and a sense of efficacy, while chronic failure stifles motivation.

3. *Power* is shown in the ability to control one's behavior and gain the respect of others. Those lacking power feel helpless and without influence.

4. *Virtue* is worthiness judged by values of one's culture and of significant others. Without feelings of worthiness, life is not spiritually fulfilling (cited in Brendtro, Brokenleg, and Van Bockern, 1990, p. 35).

The Native American values of belonging, mastery, independence, and generosity are roughly parallel to the four components of self-esteem identified by Coopersmith. They are also compatible with Maslow's theory of human needs (1954). He speculated that children and adults alike share needs to be safe and secure; to belong and to be loved; to experience self-esteem through achievement, mastery, recognition, and respect; to be autonomous; and to experience self-actualization by pursuing one's inner abilities and finding intrinsic meaning and satisfaction in what one does.

Students are not fussy about where they get their needs met. If the classroom is not the place then the school corridors will do. If the school is not the place, then the gang, the after-school job, or some other setting will be the place. Sometimes students give up on getting their needs met. When this happens they are inclined to withdraw within themselves in passive alienation or to strike out at society in violent alienation.

In traditional Native American society child rearing was widely shared. Kinship was defined biologically and tribally. This wider definition reinforced the spirit of belonging, creating a connection between community by kinship and community of place. This primary-group network of relationships made teaching values and providing caring easier, preventing, if you will, most "discipline problems" from emerging in the first place. The message for schools is clear. Emphasize the creation of classrooms in both elementary and secondary schools that resemble small family groups. Within these classrooms provide for table groupings of students. Connect these family groups into clusters to create neighborhoods of classrooms. Keep groups together for long periods of time. Remember "it takes a village to raise a child." With this kind of attitude and environment, classroom discipline problems are handled naturally as community members live their lives together.

The spirit of mastery is addressed by satisfying student needs to be competent, to achieve, and to experience success for having risen to challenges. As Brendtro and colleagues explain, "The simple wisdom of Native culture was that since all need to feel competent, all must be encouraged in their competency. Striving was for attainment of a personal goal, not being superior to one's opponent. Just as one felt ownership in the success of others, one also learned to share personal achievements with others. Success became a possession of the many, not of the privileged few" (p. 40). The message for schools is clear. Link student success to personal goals rather than comparing one student with another. Encourage cooperative endeavors. Avoid pitting one student against another. Share success. Share responsibility for success.

A powerful literature on personal causation supports the importance of cultivating a spirit of independence. Richard De Charms (1968, p. 274), for example, documents the importance of "origin" feelings in motivation. An origin is a person who believes one's behavior is determined by his or her own choosing. A "pawn" is a person who believes one's behavior is determined by external forces beyond control. Students and adults want to feel like origins and are motivated to experience those feelings. By contrast, pawn feelings encourage students to feel powerless and ineffective, thus dampening motivation. De Charms believes that students and teachers alike strive to be effective in influencing events and circumstances in their environment. When they are unsuccessful, they experience frustration and powerlessness and often become alienated from the classroom and the school.

Origin feelings are not encouraged by extrinsic rewards. Indeed the use of such rewards to get students to perform actually results in their feeling like pawns. Over time extrinsic rewards such as jelly beans, free time, prizes, and stars actually can lead to less motivation. Greene and Lepper's "felt-tipped" study (1974) is an example of the evidence that extrinsic rewards can backfire. In that study, preschool children who were motivated to draw with felt-tipped markers without extrinsic rewards became less interested in drawing once such rewards were introduced. Students, and teachers for that matter, just don't like being manipulated and over time they show it.

Further, as James Mahoney, a high school principal in Falls Village, Connecticut, points out, relying on extrinsic rewards to get students to behave or to motivate them to learn helps create a school game of winning and losing. "Children learn at an early age that they are being sorted, ranked, and classified according to 'ability' in the daily competition for schools' rewards: teacher approval, smiley faces, privileges, honors, bumper stickers, top grades, membership in the top groups. Somewhere around third or fourth grade many begin to accept the label of 'loser,' no matter how subtly it is applied, and turn off to learning. By the time they reach high school they have learned to play the game by working out unspoken agreements with their teachers." He adds, "The paradigm currently prevalent in schools, at least officially, promotes competition and excellence. But if one is to 'compete' and to 'excel,' the implication is that others must lose, even fail. In a class of 100 students graduating from an American high school this June how many regard themselves as winners? Since they all know their class rank, little is left to the imagination. Does number 35 consider herself a winner? How about number 65? Number 75 certainly thinks of himself as a loser in the game of school, and he brings this attitude with him to work." And finally, "The paradigm needs to shift from competition and excellence to cooperation and equity. In order to compete abroad, we must cooperate at home. In school, winning and losing must become irrelevant. Everyone graduating from an American high school must see himself as an active learner, a new kind of winner" (1992, p. 36).

Emphasizing intrinsic rewards is entirely consistent with Native American child-rearing philosophies. "Children were never offered prizes or rewards for doing something well. The achievement itself was the appropriate reward and to put anything above this was to plant unhealthy ideas in the minds of children and make them weak. Likewise, harsh punishment was seen as destructive" (Brendtro, Brokenleg, and Van Bockern, 1990, p. 42).

Jelly beans, prizes, and other extrinsic things can be fun and add zest to school life. Offered properly they can build camaraderie and encourage bonding. But as a general rule, extrinsic things should not be given in exchange for something in return. A class might, for example, decide to celebrate the successful completion of a project or a heroic though unsuccessful attempt at accomplishing something (such as falling short in collecting one thousand cans of food for the local mission) with a pizza party or thank their teacher with a balloon bouquet. But celebrations are just that. The quickest way to turn a fun celebration into a cold bargain is by expecting something in return.

The traditional Native American view of motivation and needs seems now to be creeping into the corporate workplace. American management is becoming suspicious of relying on extrinsic rewards to motivate workers and is searching for alternatives. The famous quality control expert W. Edwards Deming, for example, comments: "People are born with intrinsic motivation, dignity, curiosity to learn, joy in learning. The forces of destruction begin with toddlers—a prize for the best Halloween costume, grades in school, gold stars and honor to the university. On the job, people, teams, divisions are ranked—rewards for the one at the top, punishments at the bottom. MBO, quotas, incentive pay, business plans, put together separately, division by division, cause further loss, unknown and unknowable" (quoted in Senge, 1990, p. 7). Commenting on Deming's ideas Senge points out, "Ironically, by focusing on performing for someone else's approval, corporations create the very conditions that predestine them to mediocre performance" (p. 7). Both Deming and Senge would feel comfortable with the idea of classrooms as democratic communities where a shared social constitution reigns, norms are governing, motivation is intrinsic, and people are expected to respond out of felt obligations.

Instilling the spirit of generosity was a prime value in

Native American child-rearing philosophy. This value is entirely consistent with the aim of democratic community building: helping students to become active citizens and caring adults. A fundamental tenet of any democratic society is the establishment of an individual and collective responsibility for the common good — the welfare of all others in the community.

One way to instill the spirit of generosity, to teach caring, is by calling upon students to become actively involved in service projects. Even kindergartners and first-grade students can be called to service. High school students might teach residents of the local nursing home to use computers; younger children can clean their classroom, water the flowerpots in front of the school, or phone classmates who are ill. The Japanese are further ahead of us on this count. They routinely call upon students to share responsibility for caring for their schools with wonderful results. Vancouver teacher Jan Halliburton provides this account: "The schools we visited gave us the royal treatment and presented a special program in our honour. We saw firsthand the pride the students take in their schools. The public schools are maintained to a certain degree by the students themselves — they clean the rooms and the washrooms, weed the flower beds, wipe the floors down in the hallways and serve the noon meal. Tasks are assigned to every student on a rotating basis. Although some of the schools are old compared to our facilities, they are much cleaner — a reflection of the pride and respect the students have for their school" (1992, p. 3).

A service project, whether limited to in-school or community based, helps students become committed to causes beyond themselves. When caring is made part of the curriculum, students are encouraged to embrace such virtues as "courage, acceptance of responsibility, honesty, integrity, tolerance, appreciation of individual differences, and caring about others" (Carnegie, 1989, p. 26).

Asking students to care and calling on them to demonstrate this caring through service activities is a way to let them know that we need them, that they are important, that they have something to contribute, that they are carrying their own weight as members of a democratic community. Through the call for

service, each of the Native American child-rearing values—
belonging, mastery, independence, and generosity—can be
enhanced.

One advantage of *gemeinschaft* discipline strategies that
rely on classrooms and schools becoming democratic communities is that they are proactive. Aiming to establish a classroom
constitution and relying on norms, teaching active citizenship,
and seeking to develop caring adults are all ways to provide for
the belonging, mastery, independence, and generosity needs of
students. As these needs are met, fewer discipline problems are
likely to emerge and those that do emerge are handled naturally,
just the way traditional families have handled problems over
time. This is the way Marva Collins, the founder of Westside
Preparatory School in Chicago, thinks. She believes that the key
to disciplining children is empowering them.

> At Westside we teach children moral lessons about
> determination and perseverance. . . . When I'm
> dealing with a child who really wears me down, I
> tell him that I'm very upset with him, but I refuse to
> let him fail. We are on the same team, trying to
> reach the same goal. Together we can do it. Once we
> take that attitude, we see that our classrooms are
> just a bit different from those that are around
> us. . . . When I taught in a public high school for
> three years I always ate lunch with a different group
> of students whether they were in my class or not,
> until I got to know most of them. The teachers
> thought I was idiotic, but they didn't realize that it
> actually made it easier for me to teach, that before I
> could effectively discipline students, I had to earn
> their friendship and respect. When you hear a stu-
> dent say that you are the only teacher who has ever
> listened to them, then you know that you have made
> a difference [Collins, 1992, pp. 4–5].

Gesellschaft discipline strategies, on the other hand, are
reactive. Here are the rules. Here are the consequences. Break

the rules and suffer the consequences. Follow the rules and get a reward. Those with more power make the rules, decide the consequences, and dish out the rewards and punishments to those with less power. No lessons are learned. And, while a student's behavior might be modified while the system is applied in a classroom or a school, there is little guarantee that students will continue to behave when not in the classroom or the school. *Gemeinschaft* strategies seek to motivate the student from within. *Gesellschaft* strategies depend upon external motivation. Considering that from birth to age eighteen students spend roughly 9 percent of their time in school and 91 percent of their time at home, in the streets, and in employment, *gesellschaft* strategies are shortsighted, to say the least.

In a democratic community not only must students share responsibility for creating a classroom constitution and then share the obligation to live this constitution in their everyday lives, they also have a responsibility to regulate their own behavior and that of their peers. In compliance-oriented discipline strategies, and to a lesser extent in responsibility-oriented discipline strategies, everything depends on adults. Adults set up the system, decide how the system will work, and monitor the system by assuming roles as managers, arbitrators, and judges. Within this context, conflict is something to avoid for when it appears, the demands on teachers and other adults are just unbearable.

Johnson, Johnson, Dudley, and Burnett (1992) point out that most discipline problems involve conflict among students, conflict between students and teachers, and conflict between students and standards of conduct. They suggest that developing a self-regulating conflict-mediating system in a classroom can be accomplished by empowering students to be peacemakers, an idea quite consistent with the notion of classroom as democratic community.

Johnson and Johnson (1991) believe that conflict is inevitable and thus efforts should be made to turn it into an advantage. Handled correctly, they argue, conflict is essential to good teaching, to promoting caring and committed relationships among students, to promoting healthy social development, to making life more interesting and fun, to helping students understand themselves, and to helping students learn how to manage conflict constructively in their adult lives. In their words, "The energy that students put into being angry and upset could be focused on learning when conflicts are resolved constructively. The benefits gained from learning how to manage conflict constructively far outweighs the costs of learning time lost by students being upset and angry. From a cost-analysis perspective, one of the soundest investments educators and students can make in classroom and school productivity is teaching students how to manage conflict constructively" (pp. 1:9, 1:10).

To help things along the Johnsons have developed a curriculum that provides role plays and opportunities for students to learn and practice the skills needed to manage conflicts. They recommend that the process begin with the creation of a cooperative environment in the classroom. Not surprisingly, they recommend cooperative learning as one way to achieve this goal. A second step is to actually encourage intellectual controversies as part of the teaching and learning process. The Johnsons believe that controversies involving ideas encourage students to think critically and to use higher-level reasoning strategies. They learn also to prepare positions and present and advocate them in civilized ways. And they learn to respect the views of others. This emphasis on the resolution of academic controversies is good training ground for dealing with more interpersonal conflicts.

The Johnsons then encourage that students be taught how to negotiate constructive resolutions to their own conflicts that are of a more interpersonal nature. These "conflict of interests exist when the actions of one person attempting to maximize his or her wants and benefits prevent, block, or interfere with another person maximizing her or his wants and benefits. When two students both want the same library book at the same time, a conflict of interests exists" (p. 1:7).

To resolve conflicts of interest, students must be taught the procedures and skills of negotiating. When students are unable to resolve their own conflicts, they go on to the next step, which is to involve a student mediator, a neutral third party. The mediator listens carefully to both sides and helps the parties reach a just, fair, and workable solution. Peer mediation "empowers the students who sometimes feel that they are victims of the 'arbitrary' whims of the teacher. It also reduces the demand on the teacher, who can devote less time to arbitration and discipline in general, and more time to teaching" (p. 1:15). When mediation fails, the process moves on to the next step: the teacher or principal is called upon to arbitrate the conflict.

As I talk with my students and with other teachers and administrators about democratic community, some wonder whether this approach will be tough enough or whether it will become just another "permissive strategy" that will burn us in the end. This is a fair question. To answer it, I find it useful to distinguish between authoritarian and authoritative approaches to child rearing and school discipline. Dictionary definitions of *authoritarian* include references to "unquestioned obedience" and to authority coming from a "dictator" rather than from individual freedoms that require good judgment and proper action. Definitions of *authoritative*, by contrast, refer to "competent authority" and to official authority that comes from some "doctrine." Authoritative approaches tend to be more idea based, more concerned with obligations to agreements as sources of authority. In practice, they require that those in "authority" lead by reason, lead by teaching, and lead by relying on the substance of ideas rather than on raw power or on clever psychological manipulation. In many respects the authoritative approach is tougher than the authoritarian approach for it asks more from everyone and expects more from everyone.

A second question is frequently asked: Shouldn't there be some list of "cardinal sins" that are set by adults as non-negotiables for everyone to follow? The answer is yes. Though classroom constitutions ought to be developed that define standards for community members to live their lives together, it is perfectly sensible to list a handful of do's and don'ts that everyone (including adults) must adhere to. At the Duffy School in Rochester, New York, for example, community members are expected to obey the following ten commandments (Wager, 1992, p. 36):

1.   No weapons—real or toy.
2.   No pushing, tripping, hitting or fighting.

3. No swearing.
4. No threatening.
5. No insulting others.
6. Stay where adults are in charge.
7. No classroom disruption or refusal to follow adult direction.
8. Respect things that belong to others (no stealing, extorting, destroying).
9. Do not touch fire alarms; do not bring matches.
10. No alcoholic beverages, drugs or cigarettes.

As principal Barbara Wager explains, "Deciding on a handful of 'thou shalt nots' caused me to abandon my role as police chief and sheriff. I had become Moses" (p. 36).

When any of the ten commandments are broken a second time, violators are referred to a "climate committee," comprising eight to ten teacher volunteers, an administrator, and a few parents. The climate committee serves as an informal court where conflicts can be resolved. When the problem involves students and teachers, there is no guarantee that the student will automatically be found guilty or the teacher automatically absolved from blame. Though this does not happen often, sometimes teachers are found to be the source of the problem and are "told in carefully couched language that the incident might have been handled in a better way" (p. 36). When punishments must be dished out for infractions, they are not arbitrary but are natural consequences linked to what the infraction is. "A child who ripped up a stack of class compositions had the task of reproducing every one. Two children who fought in the lunchroom were afforded the pleasure of each other's company for a month of luncheons in a private, supervised place" (p. 37). Duffy's system isn't perfect but it is a step in the right direction — a step toward trying to develop discipline policies that are based on moral authority rather than psychological tricks.

Another common question is whether students have enough of an altruistic bent to respond to democratic community; are they so concerned with the satisfaction of their self-interests that they are incapable of accepting responsibility, of giving, of caring, of believing in something, and of responding morally? I try to answer this question in Chapter Four. That discussion recognized the importance of self-interest but pointed as well to another side of our human nature, one that I believe is dominant. Etzioni (1988) puts the question this way: "Are we, basically, but another species in the animal kingdom, or have we a nobler self, in continuing struggle with our baser part?" (p. 23). To answer this question I ask that we reflect on our own selves, our own motivations, and our own behavior. Think, for example, of the many occasions when we sacrifice our own self-interests for causes and ideas that we believe in and for people we care deeply about. Most of us, I believe, not only admit to this nobler self but can point to many instances from our own experience and those of others we know that demonstrate that the nobler self is alive and well.

It would be unrealistic to expect that young children should respond in the same way that older children and adults do. Nonetheless, the evidence discussed in Chapter Four suggests that this noble capacity may well be innate in the human species. In schools this noble side too often remains more potential than real. The myth of self-interest is so entrenched in our thinking and in the ways we operate in schools that it colors our view. Whenever we want something from someone, we are inclined to try to figure out how to pay for it by providing contingencies in the form of rewards and punishments.

Educational pioneer Kurt Hahn believed that students want desperately to contribute selflessly to causes they value. Students want to care, want to give, and want to serve. We can get them to respond by relying on persuasion, compulsion, or attraction. In Hahn's words: "You can preach at them: that is a hook without a worm; you can order them to volunteer: that is dishonest; you can call upon them: you are needed, and that approach will hardly ever fail" (cited in Brendtro, Brokenleg, and Van Bockern, 1990, p. 92).

Those of us who are fortunate to live in a democracy recognize the importance of active citizenship and the importance of caring for each other. Those of us who are responsible for preparing tomorrow's citizens have an obligation to teach active citizenship and caring. What better way is there to teach these values than actually living them? What better way is there for students to understand what is needed for democracy to work than for schools and classrooms to become democratic communities?

8

Becoming a Professional Community

There is a feeling in our society that professionlizing anything makes it better. But this love affair with professionalism may be fading a little. Some educators, for example, are expressing doubts about whether professionalism (at least as we have traditionally understood the concept) really fits teaching. David Coulter, an administrator in Winnipeg's Seven Oaks School District, explains: "The picture of teachers as professionals in the same sense as doctors or lawyers, dispensing education to their client-students [is not adequate]. Instead of searching for outside metaphors for schooling, perhaps we are better to return to the classroom and to the image of teacher caring for his/her students, guiding, helping them learn as a group and as individuals, using both disciplinary and pedagogical knowledge to steer a course on an educational odyssey" (1991, p. 2).

To Coulter, it is not the idea of professionalism *per se* that seems troublesome, it is the meaning we give the term. Instead of looking inward to teaching, to the kinds of relationships we have and want in schools and to the ideal of community, we have imported the meaning of professionalism from other fields. We have, for example, relied heavily on medicine as the metaphor. This metaphor focuses our attention on some dimensions of professionalism that make sense. It causes us, for example, to pay attention to the importance of developing a knowledge base and using it to inform the decisions that we make. It forces us to be concerned about developing strong preparation programs for teachers and for committing ourselves to continued professional development. And it highlights the importance of taking a problem-solving stance when planning for teaching and when dealing with issues that arise when teaching.

But the metaphor creates problems, too. It encourages us to view professionalism primarily as a technical activity involving the delivery of expert services to clients. This view shapes how we understand teaching practice. We come to believe, for example, that professionals enjoy a knowledge and skill monopoly. Teaching comes to be viewed as *instruction* involving the delivery of expert knowledge to students. During the transmission process the teacher's role is active and the student's role is passive. A contract is implied: the teacher gives expert service, the student gives submission. The teacher has the power to do, decide, and direct, and students are expected to follow.

But submission creates dependency. Students become dependent upon their teachers for everything, and this raises moral questions that must be resolved. Moral questions cause us to consider ways in which rules of ethical conduct can be added to the professional equation to round out the delivery of expertness. Fischer (1990) explains: "Experts are presumed to deliver their services to the limit of their competence, to respect the confidences granted them by their clients [parents and students, for example], and not to misuse for their own benefit the special powers given them within the boundaries of their relationship. In return, clients are expected to accept the professionals' authority in specific areas of expertise, to submit to the professionals' ministrations" (p. 358). Professionalism becomes defined as the delivery of expert service that is governed by rules of ethical conduct.

These borrowed conceptions of professionalism, however, are not always consistent with community building. Too often they:

- Encourage student-teacher relationships that are tilted in the direction of *gesellschaft*
- Emphasize the competence side of the professional ledger to the neglect of the virtuous side
- Rely on codes of conduct and rule-governed behavior to

handle ethical questions, instead of cultivating standards of
professional virtue and moral behavior

Relationships between professionals and clients are often
characterized by cordiality, decency, and good intentions. But at
the heart they must be impersonal if they are to work. A certain
distancing is required if professionals are to objectively determine client needs, to make the correct decisions, and to deliver
the most effective services. To protect the process of delivering
technical services to clients from compromise, students tend to
be viewed as cases, and this results in a tilt toward *gesellschaft*.

Competence plays an important role in any conception
of professionalism. Professionalism, after all, assumes the existence of a formidable knowledge base that informs practice.
The word "inform" rather than "prescribe" is critical in differ-
entiating between professional and technical work. In the latter,
the technician is always subordinate to the knowledge base. It
tells her or him what to do. Technical work is, in a sense, scripted
work. In the professions, by contrast, practitioners are superor-
dinate to the knowledge base. They draw upon it and are informed by it, as they make decisions about what to do and how to
do it. But how this knowledge is embodied in practice depends
on the circumstances they face. Thus professional knowledge
may exist in part before the fact. But for the most part it is
created in use as professionals make decisions about their
practice.

Even if we get the knowledge side of the ledger right,
professionalism is always more than expertise. Though gifted
safecrackers, baseball players, and hairdressers bring to their
practice high levels of expertness, we do not seriously consider
these fields to be professions. Thus expertness may be indis-
pensable, but the hallmark ingredient in defining professionalism is virtue. Virtue comes from a commitment to values
that constitute the professional ideal for any given practice.

In *After Virtue* (1981), the philosopher Alasdair MacIntyre
points out that the concept of *practice* is key to understanding
professional virtue. Virtue in a practice involves the cultivation
of specific habits of the mind, heart, and hand. It requires that

we come to think in certain ways, believe in certain things, and act accordingly. To MacIntyre, "Virtues are dispositions not only to act in particular ways, but also to feel in particular ways" (p. 140). He leads us to think of the practice of teaching as a well-defined human activity that is complex in its undertaking, that involves cooperation with others, that is aimed at accomplishing something of value, and that involves standards which define the practice. To become part of this practice, one must be willing to subject attitudes, choices, preferences, and tastes to these standards.

Standards include but always transcend competence. For example, if the practice of teaching were understood as described above, at the center would be a core of beliefs, conceptions, values, and commitments that represent an authority structure which governs what is considered good and effective and what people should and should not do in sustaining their commitments. This core would constitute the *professional ideal* toward which members will be expected to strive.

In teaching, the professional ideal is made up of four dimensions (see, for example, MacIntyre, 1981; Flores, 1988; and Noddings, 1986):

1. A commitment to practice in an exemplary way
2. A commitment to practice toward valued social ends
3. A commitment to not only one's own practice but to the practice itself
4. A commitment to the ethic of caring

Taken together the four dimensions provide the ingredients for creating a powerful norm system within a school, a system that gives direction and meaning on the one hand and represents a source of authority for what is done on the other. A commitment to exemplary practice means staying abreast of new developments, researching one's practice, and trying out new ideas. In a sense, it means accepting responsibility not only for one's own present practice but for enhancing one's future practice through professional development.

A commitment to exemplary practice translates into a

commitment to make the school a learning and inquiring community. Roland Barth (1990) speaks eloquently to this theme. He points out that too often "schools are seen as places where children learn and adults teach" (p. 50). His vision is school as a place where everyone is involved in learning and everyone is involved in teaching. "An anthropologist friend tells me that dramatic profound learning takes place in societies in which people of all ages, generations, and positions—grandmother, father, child, adolescent, hunter, cook—live, work, and learn together simultaneously. The grandfather teaches the daughter. The mother teaches the cousin. Everyone is a teacher and everyone is a learner. In many ways, schools [should] resemble these cultures" (p. 43).

Families, neighborhoods, villages, and other *gemeinschaft* images are naturally compatible with what we know about creating settings and conditions that enhance learning for both students and adults. Yet we persist in thinking about learning in accordance with the more *gesellschaft* transmission model, where experts create instructional delivery systems as a way to transmit their expertness to clients. Escaping from this thought trap, as this book argues, requires forsaking the metaphor school-as-organization for school-as-community. Becoming a learning community requires a change in the basic theory of schooling.

A community of learners, according to Barth, seem to work from the following assumptions:

> Schools have the capacity to improve themselves if the conditions are right.
>
> When the need and the purpose is there, when the conditions are right, adults and students alike learn and each energizes and contributes to the learning of the other.
>
> What needs to be improved about schools is their culture, the quality of interpersonal relationships, and the nature and quality of learning experiences.
>
> School improvement is an effort to determine and provide, from without and within, conditions un-

der which the adults and youngsters who inhabit schools will promote and sustain learning among themselves. By building community in schools we increase the likelihood that capacity will be tapped, conditions will become right, and the culture of the school will be improved [p. 45].

Learning communities are also communities of inquiry. In such communities attitudes about teaching and learning and about problem solving are different. We now rely too much on outside experts, professional staff developers, and consultants when we are in a jam or want to change things. They seem to have such easy solutions to our problems. Typically the solutions are packaged to make adoption easy. When we care deeply and are under the gun to do something these offerings seem not only compelling but irresistible.

Not to be outdone, professional organizations and academies and state and regional educational agencies sometimes join the fray either by sponsoring the packaged offerings of outside experts or by developing and marketing packaged solutions of their own. Even when we do look inward, instead of looking to the school we tend to look to the central office. Again, we rely on "experts" from outside the school to come up with the solutions and then in-service us in how these solutions are to be implemented.

Sometimes expert advice from outside sources can be helpful. This is especially the case when experts are requested by those in the school and help with problem solving on the school's terms. The focus is not on changing the school but helping the school itself change. Unfortunately, the buying of solutions has become so much a part of the school landscape that it has resulted, I fear, in a crisis of confidence. Principals and teachers often do not feel that they have the insights or the means to solve their own problems. Schools cannot become communities of learners; schools cannot become inquiring communities, unless this situation is changed.

One way to begin to change this situation is to help schools engage in school-based inquiry. Such inquiry, according to UCLA professor Jeannie Oakes (1992), is "characterized by open communication, reflection, experimentation, risk-taking, and trust among the diverse members of that school's community. . . . In stark contrast to the traditional. . . approach to school improvement—conducted by experts outside the school—this inquiry process locates the locus of change at the school itself, and grounds the effectiveness of change in the participation of those at the school in critical discourse about and practical experimentation with new practices" (p. 25).

The second dimension of the professional ideal, a commitment to practice toward valued social ends, means placing ourselves in service to students and parents and to the school and its purposes. When this ideal is in place, our work is elevated to a form of stewardship. By becoming teachers and principals, we accept the trust that parents give us to do the right thing, to give our best, to make the right calls. We treat students as we would members of our own family. We also accept the trust that our nation gives us by doing our best to prepare the next generation of its adult citizenship. Stewardship, as we shall discuss later, requires transforming teaching from an occupation to a calling.

The heart of the professional ideal in teaching may well be the third dimension, a commitment to the ethic of caring. Caring requires more than bringing state-of-the-art technical knowledge to bear in one's practice. It means doing everything possible to enhance the learning, developmental, and social needs of students as persons. The heart of caring in schools is relationships with others (teachers, parents, and students) characterized by nurturance, altruistic love, and kinshiplike connections. Berkeley professor Lynn Beck points out that caring always involves, to some degree, at least three activities: receiving the perspective of the other person, responding to the awareness that comes from receiving, and remaining in the caring relationship for a length of time (1992).

Caring is an end in itself. We care because it is good to care. But in schools as purposeful communities, caring must also be demonstrated in substantive ways that translate into student learning. This is an important point. Many teachers and principals, for example, who feel comfortable with *gesellschaft*-like schools and with views of teaching as a technical activity believe that caring too much can compromise objectivity in student-teacher relationships. This, in turn, can lead to a compromise of academic standards and ultimately to less effective student learning.

Nell Noddings (1986) thinks otherwise. To her, "Fidelity to persons does not imply that academic excellence, the acquisition of skills, or the needs of contemporary society should be of no concern. To suppose, for example, that attention to affective needs necessarily implies less time for arithmetic is simply a mistake. Such tasks can be accomplished simultaneously, but the one is undertaken in light of the other. We do not ask how we must treat children in order to get them to learn arithmetic but, rather, what effect each instructional move we consider has on the development of good persons. Our guiding principles for teaching arithmetic, or any other subject, are derived from our primary concern for the persons whom we teach, and methods of teaching are chosen in consonance with these derived principles. An ethic of caring guides us to ask, What effect will this have on the person I teach? What effect will it have on the caring community we are trying to build?" (p. 499).

We can conclude that caring equals relationships. Also, caring equals actions that enhance the school's purposes. But more important, caring equals obligations that emerge from commitments to the professional ideal and acceptance of the professional authority that results. Further, caring equals obligations that emerge from a commitment to shared community values and the moral authority that results. This conclusion leads to the next value in the professional ideal, a commitment not only to one's own practice of teaching but to the practice itself.

The philosopher Albert Flores (1988) believes that the professional ideal includes the ability "to engage in a practice informed by the virtues. . . [in a fashion that] contribute[s] as well to strengthening and enhancing the growth and development of a practice. This is because the exercise of the virtues uniquely defines our relationship with all those other practitioners with whom we share the same purposes, goals and standards of excellence, such that the singular realization of these internal goods [purposes] naturally contributes to the overall flourishing of a practice" (p. 7).

Following Flores, there is an important difference between being concerned with one's teaching practice and being concerned with the practice of teaching. The latter concern is directed to the broad issues of teaching knowledge, policy, and practice and to the practical problems and issues that teachers face every day in their classrooms and schools. If we are concerned with the practice of teaching in the school (and more broadly the practice of teaching in society itself), teaching is transformed from an individual to a collective practice. When practice is collective, successful teachers offer help to those that are having difficulties. Teachers with special insights share them with others. Success is not defined in terms of what happens in one classroom but what is happening in the school as a whole. Teachers, in other words, feel compelled to work together because of internally felt obligations.

Taken together, the values that make up the professional ideal give new meaning to professionalism. Expertness, while remaining important, is not enough. Nor is rule-governed ethical behavior that emerges from formal or implicit codes of conduct which affix penalties to violations. This new meaning of professionalism requires a transformation of one's connection to her or his work. What one does comes to be viewed as a calling rather than a job.

According to Bellah and his associates (1985), as transformation to calling takes place, a person's work becomes morally inseparable from his or her life. Teachers are not teachers only sometimes, and principals are not principals only sometimes. Whatever they are, they are everything together.

Further, what one does in work has meaning in and of itself. Teaching, for example, is not just an activity that one engages in to help students learn but it is a virtue in and of itself. Teaching is good. Being a principal is good. Sharing knowledge is good. Sharing oneself is good. Reading Shakespeare, identifying fossils, building a papier-mâché Mayan temple, painting a

portrait, and inventing a mathematical formula need no justification beyond their own doing. Helping and loving kids, or for
that matter mastering the evil-eye gaze and using it to express
displeasure with a student's behavior, need not be linked to
outcomes in order to be justified. They are values and rituals
that define us as a community.

Too often jobs, even "professional" ones, are merely means
to make a living. They are instrumental and *gesellschaft*. Within
them "the self stands apart from what it does, and its commitments remain calculated and contingent on the benefits they
deliver" (Bellah and others, 1985, p. 69). This is not the case,
however, when jobs become transformed to callings.

Redefining Colleagueship

In schools as communities the meaning of professionalism gives
equal weight to both competence and virtue. Professional virtue, as discussed above, is defined in terms of the professional
ideal. When the ideal is embraced, the meaning of colleagueship changes. Stronger ties are created that bond people together more tightly and that bind them more tightly to shared
ideals and shared traditions.

There are hazards in this new definition of colleagueship.
In many respects it bucks important strands of privacy, individualism, and competition that loom large in the cultural
makeup of American and Canadian society. But we are a complex people. We want to maintain individuality. Yet we yearn to
create and live a coherent, moral life with others.

As Bellah and his associates (1985) see it, on the one hand
we are a people committed to a brand of naked individualism
that places a premium on freedom, competition, and equal
opportunity as the means to the pursuit of happiness. On the
other hand, we abhor discontinuity, isolation, and the loss of
community that ultimately accompanies our quest for the very
freedoms we seek. We want to be left alone to do as we please but
we're not sure how to define happiness alone. We find it easier to
talk about how to get what we want than to know what it is that we
want. And though our commitment to equal opportunity is

unwavering, we are not able to imagine what a just distribution of happiness should look like. It seems that on the surface we are committed to playing on a level field where each of us is free to work out the best deals we can. By the same token, we yearn for the kinds of connections with others that give our lives direction, sense, and meaning. We need to strike out alone. But for our lives to have meaning, we need others.

This ambivalence between the value of individualism and the need for community accounts for our discomfort whenever someone suggests that teaching practice become more collective. For most of us collegiality is a great idea as long as it means liking each other but lets us continue to work separately from each other. But having the courage to take the first step toward collective practice can be richly rewarding.

This was exactly the case when a group of English and social studies teachers in the Hatzic Secondary School in Vancouver decided to work together. They weren't really sure what they were getting into and were nervous about it. It started because of their concern with high failure rates among students in their junior classes. The solution, as they saw it, was to liven up the curriculum, to invent new ways of teaching that tilted toward cooperative learning and teaming, and to emphasize performance-based assessments. But how does one do this within the traditional 5 by 8 school timetable? The answer was to invent a new one. The teachers decided to pair English and social studies classes together and have them taught by three teams composed of both social studies and English teachers. The result was not only the development of a new humanities program but a successful teaching and learning experience.

An unexpected result of moving in this direction was to discover the benefits of becoming an inquiring community, a community of learners, a community of colleagues. In the words of the humanities team, "These partnerships, although they were self selected, were entered into with some trepidation by most involved. By the end of our first month together, we knew it was going to work. By the end of our first year teaching, we couldn't imagine teaching in any other way." What was it like being a member of a teacher team? "One member, a first year teacher, said she felt lucky because of the enhanced opportunity for growth as a professional. Another member, a 20-year veteran, said it has been the most rewarding experience he has ever had in teaching. . . . Teaching with a partner opened our eyes to new ways of being a teacher. After a while, it felt odd to go to a regular classroom and teach in the traditional manner. This discovery, along with the increased success of our students, explains the expansion of the humanities program at Hatzic Secondary School. . . . Indeed. . .we are never going back" (Orme and others, 1992, p. 16).

Despite the success described above the contradictions between our need for individuality and our quest for community raise questions about the benefits of promoting such ideas as collective practice and collegiality. It does appear that when we develop conceptions of the common good and wrap them in the norms of *gemeinschaft*, the values of individuality and freedom are compromised (see, for example, Zwiebach, 1988; Flinders, 1988; Hargreaves and Tucker, 1991). No easy answers exist to this problem. Problems may be lessened, however, by including the welfare of individuals as a central value in the school's community of mind. Further, many of the *gemeinschaft* dimensions of relationships (honoring affective over neutrality; particularism over universality; diffuseness over specificity; substantive over instrumental; and altruistic love over egocentric) can offer protections to individuals. The dimensions suggest that we have to be careful that teachers are not required to unduly sacrifice their own thoughts, preferences, and styles.

Still, the community of mind that bonds community members together and binds them to a set of ideas constitutes a collective conscience (Durkheim [1893] 1964, p. 79). This conscience represents the community's "moral constitution." Being united with others in a collective conscience gives one certain rights that guarantee a sense of individualism while at the same time extracting certain community obligations.

Rights and obligations are embedded in norm systems, not rule books. The right to privacy and the obligation to help colleagues, for example, are played out in different ways, depending on one's personality, predispositions, and other personal factors. Some may choose to embody this value physically by team teaching with others. Others may choose to maintain quite separate practices while helping colleagues in other ways. Cooperative learning, the student as worker, and learning expeditions are all ideas that might be valued as good by a faculty. But the ways in which they are embodied reflect a host of individual preferences, styles, and needs.

The meaning of colleagueship implied in the professional ideal requires a new kind of relationship between and among community members, one that transcends congeniality and physical proximity. MacIntyre (1981, p. 146) describes the relationship as follows:

> A community whose shared aim is the realisation of the human good presupposes of course a wide range of agreement in that community on goods [purposes] and virtues, and it is this agreement which makes possible the kind of bond between citizens which, in Aristotle's view, constitutes a *polis*. That bond is the bond of friendship and friendship is itself a virtue. The type of friendship which Aristotle had in mind is that which embodies a shared recognition of and pursuit of a good. It is this sharing which is essential and primary to the constitution of any form of community, whether that of a household or that of a city.

Aristotle was not referring to modern versions of friendship that emphasize only emotional bonding of a psychological nature, that are therapeutic, that are based on self-interest, that resemble *gesellschaft* egocentric love. He proposed a friendship that is based on shared ideas, self-sacrifice, obligations, and duties—the *gemeinschaft* equivalent of altruistic love. MacIntyre explains:

> Friendship of course, in Aristotle's view, involves affection. But that affection arises within a relationship defined in terms of a common allegiance

and a common pursuit of goods. The affection is
secondary, which is not in the least to say unimpor-
tant. In a modern perspective affection is often the
central issue. Our friends are said to be those whom
we like, perhaps whom we like very much. "Friendship" has become for the most part the name of a
type of emotional state rather than a type of social
and political relationship [pp. 146–147].

Thus friendship might include people enjoying themselves as they work together, being useful to each other as they
engage in interdependent work, and sharing commitments to a
common good. But in redefined colleagueship, friendship must
also include helping each other to be better persons, holding up
standards for each other, and being able to count on each other
for help when needed.

The new meaning of professionalism proposed here will
very likely raise the anxiety levels of many readers. Some might
protest, "All this is okay in theory but we are just us. We don't live
in theory, we live in the world. How can we live up to the
professional ideal? It asks too much of us." Ideals are supposed
to take the high ground. They bespeak perfection. They seek to
describe events exactly as we would like them to be. But ideals
exist only in our minds. None of us can measure up to them. Still,
ideals can renew us. They can help bring us together, give us
hope, and provide us with direction. Without them we forsake
our humanness. We forsake our connections with others and our
search for a meaningful life. These are the very things that
community building seeks to provide.

Even though we fall short, our quest for the professional
ideal is a worthy end in itself. Key, I think, is to be sincere about
our ideals and to be authentic about our shortcomings as we
seek to achieve them. Fordham University professor Robert
Starratt points the way: the professional ideal "brings us full
circle at this point. Knowing our own failures to care for others,
our own immature ways of rationalizing moral choices, knowing
our own reluctance to challenge questionable school arrangements, we are able to confront the general weaknesses in the

human community. This weakness is part of being human. Despite our heroic ideals, we often act in distinctly unheroic ways. A sense of compassion is needed for those who would act ethically—compassion for himself and compassion for others. We have to extend our caring to forgiving. The forgiveness extended, we then go on with the business of making things right" (1991, p. 197).

Building community in schools is about a shared quest to do things differently, to develop new kinds of relationships, to create new ties, to make new commitments. Part of this quest is to change the meaning of professionalism. A good place to begin is to start a conversation in your own school about what it means to be a professional. At best, this conversation will expand the definition beyond expertness to virtue. We will then need to grapple with what virtue means to us, and in our own context, as we seek to do the best for kids, as we struggle to lead our lives together better. A likely outcome of this kind of inquiry is a broad commitment to the professional ideal.

9

Becoming a
Community of Learners

University of Arizona professor Gary Griffin (1991) believes that
as principals and teachers inquire together they create community. Inquiry helps them to overcome chasms caused by various
specializations of grade level and subject matter. Inquiry forces
debate among teachers about what is important. Inquiry promotes understanding and appreciation for the work of others.
Inquiry empowers teachers by promoting greater understanding of their own work. And inquiry helps principals and teachers create the ties that bond them together as a special group
and that bind them to a shared set of ideas. Inquiry, in other
words, helps principals and teachers become a community of
learners—a place, as Roland Barth reminded us in the last
chapter, where everyone is a learner and everyone is a teacher.

At its best, inquiry and learning do not recognize bureaucratic boundaries of roles and hierarchies. One must be free to
learn—free to express oneself, free to fail, free to take risks, free
to be oneself. Inquiry, for example, requires a certain openness
to new ideas, a certain willingness to suspend judgments, and a
certain readiness to travel the path that inquiry opens. Inquiring together requires true reflection and authentic dialogue.

Neither reflection nor dialogue is possible when principals tell and teachers listen, when principals teach and teachers do what is learned. Nor are reflection and dialogue possible
when someone in-services and someone else is in-serviced.
When learning takes place within the boundaries of bureaucratic roles and hierarchies, relationships inevitably become

confrontational even in the most civil of circumstances. Leaders decide what will be done and what must be learned for it to be done properly. They then carefully craft "progressive" change strategies to get teachers to cheerfully accept the new regimen. Teachers are then trained and supported as they learn how to do the new thing. And inevitably the result is that they are likely to be guarded, to respond defensively, and to strive to do what they think is expected of them—unless they can figure out ways to ignore the changes and get away with it.

Becoming a community of learners, by contrast, is an adventure not only in learning but an adventure in shared leadership and authentic relationships. It requires a certain equality and a certain willingness to know thyself better, to be open to new ideas, and to strive to become. It is an adventure in personal development. This was one of the lessons that David Hagstrom and the faculty of the Denali School in Fairbanks, Alaska, learned as they became a community of learners. They learned as well that becoming a community of learners was a journey in becoming a community by kinship, of place, or mind, and of memory.

David Hagstrom was a Chicago area elementary school principal turned University of Fairbanks professor who suddenly found himself back in the principalship. When he became principal again he brought with him four things—a lot of caring heart; the courage to know himself and to try his best; a belief that schools, particularly Alaskan schools, should strive to become extended families that included everyone who lived within the school neighborhood; and the belief that schools, particularly Alaskan schools, should provide students with a sense of place, a deep understanding in their minds and hearts of not only who they are but where they are. In his words, "If we can unlock some of the mysteries within our natural surroundings, if we can learn to appreciate the flora and fauna of those natural settings within which we live our lives, if we can begin to understand the land around us—then our social and personal existence will take on new meaning" (Hagstrom, forthcoming).

Today, the participants in the Denali School (or the Denali Project, as this turn of events has come to be called) are

building a sense of place—with all its history and culture—and
are creating an extended family. The Denali story, as told by
David Hagstrom, follows. (David Hagstrom's account of what
happened at the Denali School is summarized from his article
"Alaska's Discovery School," *Educational Leadership*, February
1992, *49*(5), pp. 23–27. He was generous in sharing several
other documents including some not yet published. Deborah
Pomeroy and Sandra Lanning also shared their insights into the
Denali story.)

> Denali Elementary School, the oldest school in
> Fairbanks, Alaska, was once described as "worn out
> and unwanted." Now it is known as "Alaska's Discov-
> ery School." The transformation occurred because
> the school and the community pulled together to
> accomplish a common goal: to make their school a
> better place for the children.
>
> In its cultural makeup, Denali Elementary is
> Alaska in microcosm: 20 percent Alaska Native
> students, 5 percent African Americans, 4 percent
> Asians, 1 percent children from Central and South
> America, and 70 percent Caucasians, who were
> born in 30 different states and 7 nations. In this
> school community, 10 percent of the parents are
> upper-middle class or above, 65 percent are middle
> class, and 25 percent of the parents earn less than
> what the federal government considers a poverty-
> level wage. Such a rich mix of socioeconomic levels,
> ethnic practices, and traditions makes the school
> interesting and, at the same time, challenges those
> of us who work here.
>
> Our adventure in shared leadership, now
> called the Denali Project, had its beginnings in a
> conversation about curriculum I had with two
> teachers and two parents just a month after I'd
> arrived. One parent asked, "How can our curricu-
> lum better reflect how our children act *outside* the
> school?" The other parent chimed in, "Our kids are

naturally explorers when they're on their own at home. Why can't the curriculum make more of that fact?" That conversation planted the seed for a new Alaskan school—new not in brick and mortar, but in spirit.

We decided to invite parents and teachers to discuss a greater alignment between the curriculum and the nature of our children. We chose 6 A.M. on Tuesdays as a meeting time. With each week, our numbers grew—first 5, then 10, then 20, and finally 40. Within a month, the "Tuesday Morning Bunch" had agreed that we wanted Denali to become "Alaska's Discovery School," a place where children and adults alike would "have the opportunity to discover...(a) the wonders of the world around them and (b) their own potential for greater human growth and development."

At the center of our mission was a desire to make Denali a math-science focus school. Those disciplines, parents and teachers believed, would give children the tools necessary to open new doors of intellectual curiosity, awaken future career possibilities, and inspire a sense of wonder about the universe beyond their school. By then, I was so caught up in the excitement of the change that was occurring that I decided to stay on at Denali, rather than return to the university.

In just four months, our group grew to include not only Denali's parents and teachers but also high school teachers, university faculty, and many community members. Out of our breakfast meetings came the following goals:

1. Teachers must become learners of mathematics and science.
2. School leadership tasks need to be shared.
3. Continued community involvement is essential.

We felt strongly that these were the best ways to bring about a more lasting change. We also felt good about our chances for success because the effort was valued by the persons who would carry it out, having originated with the Denali parents and teachers.

Like most elementary teachers, ours were well versed in the language arts, but they admitted to having little content knowledge in math and the sciences. The University of Alaska volunteered to help us by sending professors to Denali once a week to give our teachers instruction in these disciplines. During the project's first year, all teachers were released every Friday for this staff development.

At first, the professors provided background knowledge. Soon, however, the teachers were eager to translate some of this information into practice. They began asking the professors to share projects and ideas that they could use in their classroom. Before long, the university professors and our teachers were teaching side by side in the classroom. A classic example of this team teaching arrangement occurred when a university biology professor and one of our teachers shared fish dissection presentations with the intermediate grade students.

Another benefit of this collaboration for the children has been field trips to the university museum and the science department's permafrost tunnel, where our kids study soil conditions firsthand.

Just as our teachers have become learners again, so have they—along with parents—begun to share leadership tasks. For instance, teachers have been instrumental in organizing programs. Since everyone knows our vision—to become Alaska's Discovery School—each teacher has carved out a personal niche that will help get us where we want to go.

For example, our Winter Survival Program grew out of an idea by one of our 4th grade teachers, who believed that in an intense winter environment like Alaska's, students need to know how to take care of themselves if an emergency ever causes them to be stranded outdoors. Previously an outdoor education director, she taught her students how to build a lean-to, how to choose food, and how to use snow as an insulator. The learning takes place in a wooded area close to the school. Her program has since been expanded to other classes.

One of our most popular programs is a community garden, 60 feet from the school. Three years ago, a parent with a 4-H background came up with this wonderful idea. Agreeing that all kids could benefit from an understanding of how things grow, parents and community members pitched in to help.

Every child in the school has a personal plot in the garden. We take advantage of this hands-on science opportunity by coordinating our school-wide science curriculum appropriately by grade level with what's occurring in the community garden.

When school isn't in session, the 4-H Club and interested neighbors water and tend the garden. With summer temperatures in Fairbanks reaching the 80s and 90s and 22–23 hours of sunlight daily in June and July, we've been able to grow some beautiful flowers and lush vegetables: giant cabbages, carrots, beans, peas, potatoes, pumpkins, melons. At state fair competitions, we've won numerous first places. The community garden is a source of pride.

Well, this *is* what teaching is all about at

Denali. Every teacher has found an area of interest
and taken complete control so that the effort fits
our common school goal.

When most of us read success stories our first reaction is
likely to be, Well, they had strong leaders, visionaries who like
magnets were able to draw people to them and their ideas. Or
perhaps, They had leaders who led by the force of their strong
personalities. Or even, They had leaders who led because they
had clout and knew how to use it. But what about me? I am just
plain vanilla me. A "superman" of any stripe I am not. Well,
neither is David Hagstrom. He is quiet and unassuming in
appearance, soft and caring in manner. So how did he do it?

In an interview with Deborah Pomeroy (1992), David
Hagstrom comments, "I really believe it wasn't so much what I
envisioned as what they [teachers and parents] envisioned. I
think the secret to the success of the Denali Project was that this
was truly their idea" (p. 2). They created the vision, which one
teacher explains as follows: "It is not that we don't value the
typical reading and writing elementary school, it's that we want
something more for our children. We want our children to have
an 'edge' on their future. We want them to be able to handle the
challenges that will come their way. We simply believe that an
elementary school restructured around a science and math
focus makes good sense. Such a school, we believe, has the best
chance of equipping all our children for a full and satisfying
life" (Lanning, 1990, pp. 6–7).

The core of teachers who had been at Denali for several
years were competent and demonstrated a strong sense of professionalism. But the transformation to community could not
have been achieved without the emergence of a community of
mind as to what was important and what was to be, and a
commitment to inquiry that would make them a community of
learners. These were the essential ingredients needed to transform the faculty from a collection of individuals, all separately
doing the best they could, to a powerful "we" united in common
purpose and action. This vision is embodied in the following
"official" school statements ("Discovery Grant Proposal," 1989):

We call our school "Alaska's Discovery School" to emphasize the importance of discovery in our approach. We believe that all learners, whether children or adults, must discover new knowledge for themselves, and in a sense reconstruct or synthesize that knowledge anew. We want our children to be able to say, in Robert Oppenheimer's words, that they became scientists (or engineers or playwrights or whatever) because their teachers allowed them the exhilaration of their own discoveries.

The Denali Project would build a new teaching-learning model, among both children and among teachers. This model emphasizes teachers as active learners alongside their students. Teachers and students working together develop an understanding of the spirit and character of scientific inquiry and values. Students and teachers actively engage in the use of hypotheses, the collection and treatment of data, and the design of investigations [pp. 1–2, 5].

The faculty worked together and learned together, and eventually formulated these ideas into a little green booklet entitled *The Denali Discovery School Plan* that would guide their efforts over a period of seven years. Hagstrom (forthcoming) explains:

In it, we describe the curiosity we see in our children and the hopes we have for Alaska—the need we feel for having a better balance between giving and taking in our state. We describe our vision of an elementary school that captures the natural curiosity of children and creates a discovery-school focus. We list the expectations we have for changes teachers will make in the way they teach and the expectations that teachers and parents have for new learning for the children. We describe what is meant by community effort, how teachers are to become learners again, and how this community's vision is linked to the need for a massive staff development effort. The plan outlines these efforts, provides science course descriptions, contains ways to revise and align the curriculum, and lists improvements expected in student achievement and attitude. The little booklet also notes goals for each of the seven years and provides ways to evaluate progress being made with the project. It provides an outline, a timeline, and the incentive that children, teachers, and parents need to keep the school moving forward.

A math and science focus themed to making a school a discovery school can be scary to most elementary school teachers and principals. They are more comfortable with a language arts or social studies emphasis. This was the case at Denali, and thus making the vision a reality was a daunting task in both learning and living for everyone. In an interview with Deborah Pomeroy (1992, pp. 3–4), Hagstrom describes his own feelings at the time:

> Being connected with the people in education who talk about shared leadership and learning communities, what became obvious to me very early on is that (and this obliterated any concerns I had about not knowing a lot about math and science) these parents and teachers were talking about *creating a learning community.*
> I remember the light bulb went on, and I said "Hey, maybe I can take a chemistry class!" I kept thinking of ways that I could pick up on the roads not taken in my own background. I also started thinking that there were areas of science in which I'm self-taught. I'm an amateur radio operator, and as I moved up the ranks from novice to technician to general to advanced, I had to learn a lot of physics.

I also have an interest in gardening. When we started talking about a community garden, I thought that perhaps I could get out there on the tractor, be involved in the planting, and help with the greenhouse. So I guess the discovery-school idea opened up some doors about new areas in which I could learn and gave me the feeling that all of us — teachers and parents — would be learning together, with the kids watching.

When asked whether as principal he saw himself more as a learner than leader, Hagstrom responded:

Yes, I think it was at that point that there was a transfer of concepts. Perhaps up until that point, all of us involved in this Denali Project were thinking about the school as an organization. Now, all of a sudden, we were thinking about the school as a learning community.

At that point, I was able to toss off my shoulders any concerns I might have developed over the years about how principals are supposed to operate, about chains of command and bureaucracies. It was like birthing a baby. We realized we didn't have to worry about bureaucracies, directives, and the way things are usually done in schools. We just had to take care of ourselves and this new idea we'd birthed.

How does one go about creating community? What role should the principal play? Community building, in Hagstrom's words, is:

a slow process. You don't just snap your finger and make this happen. I didn't want to be considered a charismatic person who got everybody excited, so that when I disappeared, the excitement also disappeared. I was trying to figure out how you could

create a community without being a TV-evangelist-
type individual.

I decided to make a conscious effort, every
day, to try to find out about one individual in that
school community. One person a day, five persons a
week, 20 persons a month, for 10 months. . . and
this continued for a year or more. I figured if I was
able to find out what a given individual was specifically interested in and cared about, and what he or
she would like to offer to the school community,
and if I did that for one individual a day, then each
day there would be one more person who was really
turned on to what he or she could offer to that
school community. Pretty soon we would have the
nucleus of what it would take to really move the idea
forward. . . . One day it would be a student, one day
a teacher. The next day it would be a parent. Then a
neighbor across the street. The next day it would be
the postman who brought the mail at 2:30 in the
afternoon. That's how it went [pp. 6–7].

By adopting a math-science orientation, committing to
the idea of school as extended family, and committing to the
importance of building a sense of place, the people of Denali
started to find a common focus, a common dream, and common
quest that helped them to become a community of mind. They
began to create the ties all of us need that link us to something
larger than ourselves. And it is these ties that enable us to find
direction, meaning, and significance.

Teachers were less inclined to do things because the principal said so or because that was what the rules required. Instead, they began to work hard on their own learning and on
reinventing their teaching because of the obligations and commitments they felt to the ideas that they shared with their colleagues. This quest for common meaning provided the impetus
for the people of Denali to take the learning plunge.

Learning together helped develop special bonds between
principal and teachers, among teachers, between teachers and

principals, among students, and between adults and students. *Gemeinschaft* bonds. Bonds of kinship. Bonds of caring. Bonds of commitment. Bonds of altruistic love. Bonds that define the school as a "we" united in common purpose. David Hagstrom describes these relationships:

> For me, the days I served as principal at Denali have been the most special of my life. When I came to this school community, I was introduced to the "Denali Family"—and a true family it's been for me. In my opinion, the Denali staff is a total caring team—unified in their concern for the children. And yet the staff has become that strong team because of the separate and individual talents and interests represented within the total faculty group. Listening to first one person and then the next, talking about what's really "important," I know that we just had to get some of this individual wisdom on paper [Denali Elementary School, 1991].

The result was a little booklet entitled "A Collection of Thoughts to Live By" (Denali Elementary School, 1991). The thoughts of Denali teachers were collected and edited by a retired Fairbanks teacher who interviewed each member of the Denali staff. Here are a few examples of what the teachers had to say:

> I want to give special love to our special kids. A little help will give them such a good start for their lives. Anything can be conquered if we have hope. A cheerful attitude helps when things don't just go right or the way we wanted them to go. I think it is important to be faithful and loyal to each other. Just by watching us, our students will learn a sense of responsibility. They learn by our example.
> — Ingeborg Finnesty

> I believe in a sensible approach to life with a willingness to take some detours. I think we need to

have a sense of where we are going. . . to have a
purpose. . . a direction. While we are figuring out
what to do next, we will make mistakes. Once I
heard a saying that went like this: Anything worth
doing is worth doing poorly — at least for a little
while.

—Saramarie Gislason

Every day I try just a little bit harder to be what I can
be. I want the students to know that I care and that I
understand when they are going through difficult
times. I love the people in this school. I feel like I
belong in this group.

—Kym Pihlaja

Our students are going to be the citizens who grow
up and take care of the earth. I want them to know
that they have a responsibility to develop strong
skills and qualities to take them into their future. I
want them to think of me as a tough teacher who
loved them — who demanded a lot and made them
work hard.

—Deb Wilkinson

I want my students to love and respect themselves,
each other, and the planet. I wish to create an
atmosphere that is comfortable, warm, loving and
accepting. In this environment, students will have
positive learning experiences.

—Katie Brown

I like to be there on the sidelines for my kids, to help
them find joy around them and in themselves.
When things get tough we need to draw on that
inner reserve and know that we can do it. It is easy
to get bogged down with the day-to-day responsibilities. We need to remember to relax more and enjoy
each other.

—Katharine Weber-Baker

I believe that a sense of trust is really important. I want my students to know that I will go to bat for them—no matter what the cost. It is important to be able to keep a confidence. Each child is a gift and we need to be grateful for our experiences together. Kids tend to live up to being valued. It is important to be encouraging—to help kids blossom and expand beyond. We need to realize that ideas are everywhere. It is wonderful to capture the moments of high energy. I want to treasure the moments with my students.

—Sue Mullen

Communicating is very important. It is important to keep our family ties and offer each other guidance, love and respect. Families are responsible for helping children reach their goals and guide their attitudes. It is only natural that we care about each other and try to recognize the needs of our children. I want our school to be a safe place where children feel cared for and comfortable learning. I want things to be fair and people to be encouraged to come to terms with the courses our lives take.

—Cheryl R.

I hope my students remember that they are loved. I try to express fairness and warmth as we learn our lessons together. Love is a decision you have control of.

—Richard J. Davis

The lesson for all of us from the Denali story is a simple one: as we learn together and as we inquire together, we create the ties that enable us to become a learning community. The magic of being a learning community is summed up by Deborah Zuberbueler, principal of the Stinson Middle School in San Antonio, Texas (Albritton, Burns, Franz, and Tilly, 1991, p. 4):

If we want the kids to take ownership in their own learning, they have to see us—the faculty and administration—doing just that. When they see us taking risks and exploring new ideas, they'll follow suit. That's when it gets exciting. We're learning, they're learning, everybody's learning.

10

Becoming a
Community of Leaders

It is easier to feel comfortable with the idea that schools should become communities of learners than that they should become communities of leaders. Learning together makes sense, but leading together defies some of the laws of leadership that we have come to accept. The literature, for example, frequently encourages us to provide strong and direct leadership in making schools effective. As a result, we have come to view leadership as part of an "interaction-influence system" within which the leader, acting individually, interacts with others in an effort to influence what they think and do (see, for example, Kellerman, 1984; Yukel, 1989).

Within this view, leaders may have lofty visions and may want to do the right thing but exercising leadership still means controlling events and people in a way that makes things come out the way leaders think they should. Progressive leaders, however, are not dictatorial. Instead, they share some of their responsibility for leadership with others and delegate some of their authority to others. Doing so, it is believed, increases the

Note: Unless indicated otherwise, all references to the Jackson-Keller School are based on my personal field notes and gleaned from extensive formal and informal interviews with Jackson-Keller staff. I am particularly indebted to the principal, Alicia Thomas, and to teachers Victor Herrera, Kristina McDaniel, Krista Kirton, and Kristin Shelton for their insight and support. Trinity faculty members Rose Rudnitski and Shari Albright were also helpful. Finally, I rely heavily on insights from Trinity colleague Margaret Burns, who spent many hours during the fall semester of 1992 in the school. Burns wrote the Jackson-Keller story that is included in this chapter.

likelihood that others will respond better and thus will be more likely to do what the leader thinks is good for the school.

Community building changes all this. What matters most is what the community together shares, what the community together believes in, and what the community together wants to accomplish. And this shared idea structure, this community of mind, becomes the primary source of authority for what people do. Principals and teachers together are followers of the dream, committed to making it real. And leadership is nothing more than a means to make things happen. Since not only the principal but all the followers have equal obligation to embody community values, principal and teachers together must share equally in the obligations to lead.

In communities leadership is not defined as the exercise of power over others. Instead, it is the exercise of wit and will, principle and passion, time and talent, and purpose and power in a way that allows the group to increase the likelihood that shared goals will be accomplished. In communities, leadership as power *over* events and people is redefined to become leadership as power *to* accomplish shared goals. And when this leadership is exercised by everyone on behalf of what is shared, the school becomes a community of leaders.

Roland Barth (1990, p. 124), explains the difference:

> As principal, I used to think that I shared leadership. I did. Or I should say I went as far as I could go or felt the school could go. But reflecting a decade later on my leadership, I see that I stopped well short of a community of leaders. Leadership for me was delegating, giving away, or sharing participation in important decisions to others as long as the curriculum, pupil achievement, staff development, and of course stability were not much altered. Now I see it differently. Rather, my vision for a school is a place whose very mission is to ensure that students, parents, teachers and principals all become school leaders in some ways and at some times. Leadership is making the things happen that you believe

in or envision. Everyone deserves a chance. Schools can help all adults and youngsters who reside there learn how to lead and enjoy the recognition, satis- faction, and influence that come from serving the common interests as well as one's self-interest.

The teachers at the Jackson-Keller School in San Antonio, Texas, have struggled with what it means to be a community of leaders. Working together, this is what they came up with:

- Each are open to others' ideas which makes it easy for them to work together — don't look for glory as you share.
- Having to go back to square one — be flexible — reteach.
- Open-minded — let kids be leaders — let teachers be learners.
- Updated atmosphere — understanding that learning is a life-long endeavor.
- Always be willing to try something and share.
- Supportive environment.
- Never any closure.
- Best leaders are the best servants.
- Leaders depend on expertise, not position.
- Share our knowledge and skill with children before they leave our community.
- Everyone contributes and gets a turn.
- Learning and leading is equitable.

The Jackson-Keller motto is "Everything that we do, we do for the children." School life revolves around two broad goals:

1. At Jackson-Keller we will establish a community of lifelong learners and leaders in a way that fosters the growth of the whole child through base groups, adult collegiality and cooperation, parent involvement, and cooperation and con- flict resolution.
2. At Jackson-Keller we will develop an integrated, thematic curriculum focusing on language development, and the

acquisition and transfer of academic skills, concepts, problem solving and processes.

Key to community building at Jackson-Keller was a decision the faculty made in the spring of 1992 to organize the school into five mixed-grade-level families or "base groups," each composed of grades K–5 or 1–5 and each sharing a common space. When students begin their studies at Jackson-Keller they join one of the five families and stay in that family for the duration. Within each family teachers plan together and work together, classrooms are frequently joined, and students are encouraged to relate to each other as members of an extended family. The older children, for example, walk the younger ones to the buses as an older sibling would a younger. Base groups provide the kind of sustained intimacy, cooperation, and caring that help create a community of kinship and a community by place.

The Jackson-Keller faculty made a public commitment to become colleagues and to accept all the burdens, obligations, and responsibilities that this commitment entails. To them, collegiality means:

> Working together — sharing
> Peer acceptance
> Supporting each other
> Cooperative not competitive
> Giving/taking equally
> Being united
> Taking time to listen
> No fear of ridicule
> Being honest, respecting opinion
> Accepting honest criticism
> Working toward common goal/vision

Teachers become colleagues when they share a common quest, are a part of a common tradition, and are committed to help and care for each other. But collegiality also requires a kind of authenticity that allows teachers to be themselves and to take risks, knowing that whatever the outcome they will still be accepted. Risk taking to the Jackson-Keller faculty means:

- It should not be looked at as a failure but rather a learning experience, regardless of the outcome.
- Going beyond the "norm" and being open to new ideas.
- Fear and excitement at the same time.
- Exploring uncharted waters: sometimes sinking, sometimes swimming, but always learning a lesson.
- Assuming responsibility — flexibility — reaching new heights.
- Going out on a limb with a safety net and being allowed to fall.
- Going beyond what you feel you can do.
- Believing in yourself.
- "Going for it."
- Doing things you haven't done before, falling out of your mold, not getting stale.
- Gambling to go beyond mediocrity.
- Trying new methods/approaches — being able to accept the consequences.

Jackson-Keller's commitment to parent involvement has a long history. Parents are highly visible in the school; so are teachers in the recreation rooms of neighboring apartment complexes and in the homes of students. But things were different when the school was reopened in 1988, after being closed for three years. Rudnitski (1992) reports that the first open house for parents that year was "a party to which nobody came."

One of the first goals that the faculty members set for themselves during that first year was to make the school an inviting place for students. "They would always be polite and warm and speak to parents at *their* convenience and not at the convenience of the school staff. If a parent came in unannounced with a concern, the teacher would speak to the parent immediately and set up an appointment for a longer conversation. The staff was involved in the plan. If *any* parent came in or called, the secretaries and other staff were committed to welcoming that person and making them feel at home" (Rudnitski, 1992, p. 5).

At Jackson-Keller the teachers have committed themselves to creating the kind of atmosphere that fosters citizenship, cooperation, and self-esteem in not only children but parents as well. They call home routinely to report good behavior. They learn the parents' work schedule and go out of their way to contact parents at convenient times. And "each teacher keeps a Parent Involvement Profile in his/her planbook on which he/she keeps track of the involvement of the parent/caregivers of each child throughout the school year" (Rudnitski, p. 5).

In 1992, the Jackson-Keller PTA won an award for having the highest increase in enrollment. In addition to PTA meetings there is at least one informal gathering for parents each month. There is a Muffins for Mom Day, Doughnuts for Dad Day, and Goodies for Grandparents Day. A Parent Involvement Committee, which includes parents and teachers, plans and coordinates the many parent programs. A Parent-to-Parent program helps parents help each other. Parents and children together take responsibility for decorating the big bulletin board that hangs just outside the school cafeteria.

In the spring of 1991 the school sent a questionnaire home to parents asking for their opinions about the school. Rudnitski reports than an overwhelming majority of parents cited the teacher as the thing that made them happy with the school. Among the testimonials they received were the following:

> To know that my daughter has the most beautiful teachers giving her confidence and much patience; giving her security within herself in order to continue succeeding in her studies.

> The group of teachers is proficient at teaching a person with little knowledge of the English language, especially my child's teacher.

> The teacher is very comprehensive with the children and she is very friendly with us.

We love Jackson-Keller! Meeting with the teacher
for the first time and knowing that my kid has a
beautiful, fantastic with children teacher! Fantastic
school! The teacher's total dedication to the child,
not only their three Rs, but the *knowledge* of LIFE —
from their own feelings [self-esteem] to the *needs of
others* coming first. I don't know if other schools
have teachers like this! [pp. 8–9].

We went to two other schools. We decided if this one
didn't work out, we'd send our children to [a Catholic school] we heard was a very good school. We
came, and we have stayed. We love it. The teachers
who are here are here because they want to be here.
They really care about the kids. They're here no
matter what time you come, seven-fifteen in the
morning or six at night [p. 10].

Jackson-Keller is committed to the principles of cooperative learning and last year became interested in the peacemaking curriculum developed by the Johnsons (Johnson and Johnson, 1991)—both seeds planted by the principal. A cooperative
learning team made up of four teachers has researched the topic
and has provided workshops for colleagues on cooperative
learning and students as peacemakers.

In efforts to meet the second goal, to develop an integrated thematic curriculum focusing on language development,
the Jackson-Keller faculty members have embarked on an ambitious curriculum development project. They are working with
Ernest Boyer and his staff from the Carnegie Foundation to
make Jackson-Keller the first basic school. The basic school is a
new design for elementary schools being proposed by the Carnegie Foundation for the Advancement of Teaching.

When a key curriculum consultant from Carnegie noti-
fied the school that she would be unable to lead a scheduled two-
day workshop on developing the new basic-school curriculum,
the principal and a group of teachers organized the sessions
themselves. The teachers dove into the work, figured things out

for themselves, and using themselves as resources began the curriculum development work with great success. These two days were a celebration of learning and leadership.

The faculty also tackled on its own what it means to be a basic school. Boyer provided principal Alicia Thomas with an advance copy of his book outlining the theory and structure of the basic school. Mrs. Thomas asked the teachers to read the book in pairs. Each member of the pair then interviewed the other and wrote up what was important to the other. These meanings were shared among the faculty and a booklet of meanings, "The Important Book," was prepared and distributed. Mrs. Thomas commented, "I just cried when I read it!" As the faculty struggles to become a basic school, it can refer to this important book to help answer such questions as: What does the basic school mean to us? How does the basic school fit our conception of what we want and what we believe? Two excerpts from the booklet follow:

> For Amy Jo the important thing about the chapter "Community: A Shared Vision" is the development of shared goals within a community.
> The goals drive the school in an effort to build a community.
> Schools are small.
> Connections form with a preschool.
> Emphasis is placed on the best aspects of our humanity.
> Time is an important factor to build traditions, form links and accomplish goals.
> But for Amy Jo the important thing about the chapter "Community: A Shared Vision" is the development of shared goals within a community.
>
> For Krista the important thing about the chapter "Schedule: A New Calendar and Clock" is that children would see the school as an extension of their family, not a cold institution.
> It provides day care with skilled caretakers who

guide the children to productive play and creates an enriching environment.
It would create a more open and friendly place
where parents would feel at home.
It would help give teachers the authority needed to
individualize instruction and take care of basic
needs on campus.
But for Krista the important thing about the chapter "Schedule: A New Calendar and Clock" is that
children would see the school as an extension of
their family, not a cold institution.

What the staff was able to accomplish on its own is a
demonstration of the reality that Jackson-Keller is not only
becoming a community of leaders but a community in all its
forms. At the heart of implementing both of Jackson-Keller's
goals is building relationships. Principal Alicia Thomas puts it
this way, "We are committed to building relationships within the
curriculum, with each other, with parents, and with our
community."

Jackson-Keller was not always what it is today. In 1988, it
started out as a caring community committed to loving and
serving children and their parents. But much of what went on at
Jackson-Keller in its early years might be characterized more as
"parallel play" by a collection of "I's" than unified action by a
faculty "we." The story that appears below, told by Margaret
Burns, describes how Jackson-Keller changed from being a collection of caring individuals to being a community of mind, a
community of learners, and a community of leaders. The story
illustrates, as well, the fine line that exists between learning and
leading. Becoming a community of leaders requires learning
together. And learning together required that the responsibilities of leadership be shared.

Thirty years ago, Jackson-Keller Elementary School in
San Antonio, Texas, was built to meet the needs of a primarily
affluent, Anglo neighborhood. The 70s and 80s brought with
them a substantial amount of commercial growth to the area,

moving the middle class to suburban subdivisions outside the central loop of the city. In 1985 the district was forced to close JK due to an ever-increasing decline in its enrollment.

After careful consideration and considerable concern voiced by neighborhood parents centered around issues such as school boundaries and busing, the school was reopened in 1988. These same school doors reopened to a neighborhood whose demographics had changed significantly and to a community whose needs and priorities had shifted. 1988 saw 380 pupils, 63% of whom were Hispanic, 33% Anglo, 3% African-American, and 1% Other. The second year, the population grew to 474 students, with 65% qualifying for free or reduced lunch, and one-third qualifying for at-risk status (Rudnitski, 1992). Continuing to grow each year, the school population currently stands at 547, with 70% qualifying for free or reduced lunches and one-third classified as at-risk. Despite such challenges, the principal and faculty of JK Elementary are working to provide a safe, caring learning community where individual differences are celebrated and where all children can succeed. But, exactly how are they accomplishing such a worthwhile task?

From the outside, JK Elementary School looks like any other aging urban campus. The main building has long since been outgrown; thus, it is surrounded by portable buildings which house varying grade levels and pull out programs. A large storage garage has been converted into a gymnasium used for physical education classes and recess periods hampered by inclement weather. Although the school is located on a busy street and near a main thoroughfare, the entire playground area is safely fenced. A policeman, the principal and the assistant principal maintain safety in front of the school both before and after classes. Despite limited parking space, the staff has become rather innovative in creating acceptable parking areas, thus making it possible for parents and students to "touch base" with the principals and teachers at the school.

The grounds of the school are neat and clean. Both custodians and neighboring high school students help keep the area clear of trash and clutter. The custodians are heavily invested in their school, and proud of their work. They carefully watch over the grounds, insuring a safe place for children to be. They go the extra mile to help teachers and the principal in any way they can, and they do their work with spirit and intensity. In addition, students and teachers alike take pride in their campus and pitch in whenever they can. Large potted plants have been placed out near the entrances to the portable buildings, and a courtyard currently houses a vegetable garden, giving the school a very "homey" feel.

Inside JK is a wonderful world of stimulating sights, sounds, and textures. A large wooden rabbit (JK's mascot) greets each visitor at the door with a plastic board listing the activities for the day. The hallway walls are brightly decorated with art-work, and painted handprints of the first group of students that reopened JK in 1988 line the top of the walls as a border.

It is obvious that in every aspect of the school, children are the focus and celebration. The office area is the first room one encounters when entering the building. This is no ordinary office. Rather than cold, impersonal furniture in an isolated area, there are "squishy" comfortable couches, area rugs, small chairs for children, and puzzles and books on the end tables. A cheery, helpful office staff is eager to answer questions or give directions, making visitors feel like guests in someone's home. Both adults and children experience the same sense of welcome there. This office area is always abustle with activity. Not only is this where the principals' offices, secretaries, and switchboard are located, but it houses the nurse's office, teachers' lounge, telephone area, and mail boxes. This is also where parent volun-teers and PTA members work on projects for the school. The principal's office is modest but cheerful, filled with books, me-mentos, and children's art. The office area belongs to everyone.

The library is located right in the center of the school with no walls surrounding it, allowing easy access to all. Shelves full of books are found there, as well as audio/video equipment, re-source materials for teachers, and two pet birds named Mary and Johna (the original names were Mary and John until they both laid eggs!) known to spontaneously break into song at times. It is an area that encourages and cultivates exploration and inquiry from children and adults alike.

The classrooms are magical. Each room has a personality all its own. Teachers have taken time to sew curtains in bright prints for their windows, to construct extensive artwork using school mottos and learning concepts, and in one case even to build a wooden loft/playhouse for kindergarten children that changes its face and purpose according to the topics or units being studied. The teachers have invested in their classrooms the way they would invest in a home, insuring comfort, safety, and accommodation for the children in a stimulating, inquisitive atmosphere.

Kristy, a first-grade teacher at JK, sums her commitment to her students up this way, "We get involved in the kids, I mean deeply involved. Here we love the kids. It's like a fever and everyone has it!" When Kristy was asked whether the school where she had previously worked cared about kids, she explained, "Yea, sure they did, but it was different. They were more impersonal, more sort of objective, if you know what I mean."

The learning environment and conditions are important. But it is the people of JK who are the foundation of this school, a foundation laid back in 1988. Upon JK's reopening, an alliance was formed between the school and a nearby university that was implementing a five-year teacher preparation program and looking for opportunities to be involved with innovative schools. Alicia Thomas was appointed the principal of the newly reopened school. With the university's support, Mrs. Thomas carefully and thoughtfully interviewed and selected every staff member who was to teach or work at JK. Her guiding principles were to find professionals who not only knew teaching and understood children and how they learn, but who were caring professionals. She wanted teachers who had a sincere love and concern for children. She felt that such an elevated level of caring was a necessary factor for setting an appropriate climate for the "new" school. Two of her faculty choices were recent graduates of the university's education department. The remaining selections were made from applicants across the city who knew that Mrs. Thomas wanted JK to be a special place characterized by caring and innovation.

With a faculty and staff in place and a strong leader at the helm, JK set off to chart its course as a school that cared for children. Teachers were teaching, children were learning, and the neighborhood seemed pleased with what the school was providing for its students. To foster parental involvement, teachers set up family visitation times in the evenings in the area apartment complex recreational rooms in order to get parents to view the school as an inviting rather than intimidating place. Teachers cultivated relationships among themselves by celebrating birthdays, personal accomplishments, and academic and professional awards. Teachers knew when students were experiencing family difficulties at home and were attuned to how recognition of these personal needs would be beneficial to the child's learning experience in the classroom. It appeared as though everything was in place and things could not have been better. But this was not the case!

By the fall of 1991, teachers at JK began to get restless. They had entered JK in 1988 with the understanding that innovative practices would be taking place there. And *individually* they knew that they were doing good things for kids, providing them with a wonderful sense of support and safety. But something was missing! As one teacher explained, "We had stopped to ask ourselves if we were doing anything differently from other schools. Most of us felt like the answer was no." It was this eye-opening realization that ignited conversations about what JK really wanted to accomplish as a school. Teachers have noted that such communication began in small groups in the hallways, teachers' lounge, and between colleagues in empty classrooms.

As a parallel to these discussions, several faculty members were pursuing master's degrees at the alliance university. Here, they had an opportunity to talk together about some of the ideas discussed in their courses. They brought some of these ideas back to JK and contributed together to the ongoing discussions about what the faculty saw as their vision for the school. Because of the close relationship that existed between the school and the university, and the warm interpersonal climate that characterized JK, this group of teachers felt confident in their ability to open a dialogue with their principal and hopefully bridge any gaps that might exist between them. They were motivated to play a pivotal role in moving the faculty's ongoing conversations from the hallway to an open forum, and that is exactly what happened.

Faculty and staff at JK report that the fall of 1991 was a time of uncertainty and upheaval. By the latter half of the semester, faculty meetings were consumed by individuals expressing dreams and ideas about what JK's focus should be, as well as fears and concerns about taking risks and doing things differently at the school. Ideas and practices were examined individually and collectively, in fact so closely at times that staff members were often unsure that a common ground existed.

It was at this time that Alicia Thomas began to be challenged as a leader. She had maintained a nurturing role over the years, modeling the caring attitude she felt was so important in a school. She was well-respected and admired by the faculty for her dedication to children. However, as the faculty began its press for change, they also began to press Mrs. Thomas to lead them in their quest and to assume different roles. This often involved challenging district policies and procedures, extensive reading of professional journals and literature, putting in long hours and conducting very involved individual and group meetings both at and away from JK.

Mrs. Thomas met this challenge. After much researching and soul-searching, she used the fall of 1991 as an opportunity to extend an invitation to each teacher and staff member to share his/her personal visions for what they wanted JK to look like as a school. This was facilitated by the consideration of three important questions:

1.   What things can we celebrate about JK?
2.   What now needs our attention?
3.   If we're proactive, we don't just complain. What do we do about them?

These questions were posed by Mrs. Thomas at a faculty meeting where individuals responded in small groups, allowing each person's ideas to be heard. The small groups then shared the responses with the larger group, and these responses were scribed on large charts for the faculty to consider and reflect upon. Mrs. Thomas explains, "We thought it was important to begin with the positives before moving towards the areas we wanted to change." JK was taking its first step toward developing a collective vision. This process also fostered a genuine mutual respect for other colleagues' ideas, breaking down many of the professional barriers that had some faculty members feeling isolated. The fall semester came to a close with the Christmas holidays and a renewed commitment to work on solutions and resolutions for the new year.

Action was the agenda for 1992! The JK faculty returned to school ready to work on their cohesiveness as a group of colleagues, not just friends. After reviewing the charts listing prioritized needs from the fall, Mrs. Thomas arranged for a weekend retreat away from school where the faculty could work on bonding issues, but even more importantly where they could have fun together. In the fall, teachers had expressed a desire to work together, take time to renew themselves, and as one teacher expressed, "We need to have fun. Otherwise it's tough to come to work everyday." The retreat was a crucial step toward being made aware of and meeting these needs.

Further examination of the charts from the fall revealed the faculty's collective desire to work toward integrated thematic units, small self-contained classrooms, the development of vertically aligned "family" groups, peacemaking, and continued emphasis on parental involvement. With these directives now in focus, Mrs. Thomas began formulating a framework in which to guide her faculty toward implementation of these changes. She decided to use *The Wizard of Oz* and the symbolic strength of the yellow brick road and Emerald City as guiding ideas to represent JK's journey of growth and change. She felt it important to provide a familiar and comfortable framework during a time of much uncertainty and change. Throughout the spring semester, the characteristics and components of Oz were used to discuss such weighty issues as paradigm shifts, belief systems, and decision-making/leadership responsibilities. In addition, pertinent journal articles, inspirational stories, and applicable quotes such as this one by Bernice McCarthy, "All life's decisions must ultimately rest on how well we answer the question—How will this help the children? All the children" were used to maintain a common school perspective and value system.

While it would seem quite a lofty goal in and of itself working to establish a unified practice as a faculty, it was just as important to involve other members of the JK learning community. These members included parents, and even administrators from the central office. Parents were kept informed through informational meetings, written bulletins, and one-on-one dialogues with principals and faculty. Frequent invitations to visit JK were extended to central office staff, making them feel a part of what was emerging at JK. The result was some wonderful support from these people, signifying their commitment to JK.

By spring, JK had made a great deal of progress in developing a new sense of itself and in formulating plans for making their vision a reality. This progress took tremendous dedication and effort. But the gains could not be made without some pain. The teachers and the principal had taken quite a risk. Self and collective inquiry were scary. But the result was the clarity and focus that had previously been lacking. This focus translated into a significant commitment to the development of one integrated thematic unit for the 1992–93 academic year, the adoption of an activities book, the implementation of a peacemaking curriculum, the formation of "family" groups beginning with the arrangement of room locations in the school centered around these families, and renewed commitment to parental involvement with the school building as homebase for this effort.

With a clear vision and mission in hand, Mrs. Thomas and the teachers were ready to translate their ideas into specific actions, when an interesting development occurred. Mrs. Thomas was contacted by Dr. Ernest Boyer of the Carnegie Foundation about JK becoming involved in one of his projects. Boyer and his colleagues at Carnegie had been working on a new design for the elementary school. Called the Basic School, the design called for an emphasis on language development, an interdisciplinary curriculum organized around eight commonalities of humankind, closer and more sustained grouping patterns for students, a spiral curriculum revolving around key themes, experiential learning, and new forms of assessment. Boyer was looking for schools willing to implement the Basic model with the vision that they might become lighthouse schools.

Perhaps in 1988, Mrs. Thomas might have made the decision as to whether to join forces with Boyer or not alone. But not in 1991. The idea was presented to the faculty. Mrs. Thomas has openly described the JK faculty as strong-willed and opinionated, and in this case the faculty was true to form. While some schools would have immediately jumped at an opportunity to work with such a distinguished organization, the JK faculty was more concerned with what was best for *their* students than what was best for Carnegie. They asked for illustrations of the basic ideas, specific written descriptions of the plan, verbal explanations of the guiding principles of the Basic School, and cross referenced all this information with the ideas they had generated earlier on their own. Were their goals and beliefs and the Basic School's goals and beliefs compatible? It appeared that they were. Thus, after careful consideration, the faculty collectively committed itself to becoming the first Basic School. And today they are working closely with Dr. Boyer and the Carnegie staff to best represent and meet the needs of their community through the utilization of the Basic School concept. Their growth is truly a wonderful thing to observe.

This newly established sense of community not only has given JK a platform which helps shape their decisions but is translated through and exemplified by their everyday relationships and actions. There are too many examples to mention, but here are just a few. While some may on the surface seem weightier than others, it would seem that each is an integral part of the traditions and practices that bonds this community together and that binds them to a common set of ideas.

The mascot at JK is the jackrabbit. This friendly symbol is found throughout the school halls and office area. Students even use a "rabbit wave" to quietly communicate a greeting by placing their fore and middle fingers in the shape of rabbit ears.

The entire school is vertically aligned into families who act as a support system for its teacher and student members alike. Families have tutorial study sessions together, joint projects, and even field trip experiences, allowing for a true sense of connectedness between grade levels. This alignment also provides "connections" for kids through cross-grade tutoring and buddy systems. Kids know all of the K–5 teachers because they remain in their families throughout their school lives at JK. Jennifer, a first-grader at the school best represented this idea when one morning while entering school she stopped in front of Mrs. Thomas. While pointing to another adult across the sidewalk, she emphatically stated, "Mrs. Thomas, there is my fifth-grade teacher."

Numerous before-school, after-school, and enrichment activities are organized to encourage a comfortable, supportive atmosphere in the school for students and their parents. Book fairs, arts and crafts workshops, an active parent volunteer program, and parent/community member reading times are just a few of the possibilities. Everyone feels a part of the school. As one parent observed, "I came into JK with one child and left with 550!"

The fifth grade classes make a field trip to see a live presentation of the Nutcracker ballet and are taken to a restaurant that overlooks the city for lunch, allowing room for a personal growth activity that many of the children would otherwise be deprived of.

The school as a whole is committed to extensive recycling of many materials, lining the hallways with recycling bins for easy use by school members.

Collectively JK faculty and students constructed a large get-well-soon banner signed by each school member for one of their children who had developed cancer and was having to miss a great deal of school to undergo extensive treatments.

Beginning in 1988, it was obvious that the faculty and staff of JK were struggling to create a caring school. They cared deeply for their students and for parents too. But no matter how much caring was emphasized, the school seemed still to be a structure housing individual cubicles of children and adults working in isolation. It seemed more significant to view the school as an extension of the family—a place where people not only unconditionally cared for one another, but one where people unconditionally worked together, inquired together, struggled together to become a "we" together. A place where adults and children both felt safe and comfortable enough to strive for success. A place where mutual respect is a priority. And a place where inquiry and reflection for the entire community is valued.

By 1991 JK had become a purposeful community, an inquiring community, and a professional community as well. Together the principal and teachers are working to establish a climate conducive to emotional risk-taking. A place where students, teachers, and administrators alike have the courage to express their feelings about life at JK and to contemplate openly their actions and practices as ways of conveying those feelings. They are challenging themselves to work toward a common belief system, no matter what it takes. And as they do, they are becoming a community of leaders. The following quote, circulated by Mrs. Thomas, captures the spirit:

"The future is not some place we are going to, but one we are creating. The paths are not to be found, but made, and the activity of making them changes both the maker and the destination"—John Schaar.

I remember walking through the Jackson-Keller School in 1988 and was struck by the warmth and friendly interpersonal climate that I found everywhere. When Jackson-Keller reopened, the new principal, Alicia Thomas, had a vision: to create a school that would be a caring place for students. And she carefully selected a faculty that would fill the bill. Her strengths, as a leader, were focused on encouraging, motivating, and building up the faculty and she did this by caring for them.

The teachers responded to her leadership with loyalty and appreciation and worked hard to be good and caring teachers. Jackson-Keller was a good school. Still, something was missing. Despite the magic of warmth, this faculty had much more of its talents to develop, to give, and to share.

Like a giant awakening from a slumber, there was a reawakening within this faculty as members began to push the

principal and themselves for more. Though at first Alicia
Thomas was nervous about this and fearful that her own leadership authority might be compromised, she began to respond to
these urges and indeed to nurture them. The result was the
emergence of a set of conceptions and commitments—a shared
vision, if you will—that laid the platform for what would become
the school's mission.

In the language of community building, Thomas was able
to bring the kinds of kinship ties to Jackson-Keller that laid the
groundwork for the faculty to develop among themselves a
community of mind. And the result was greater bonding among
the faculty on the one hand and on the other the kind of binding
to a set of ideas, conceptions, and values that would not only
motivate them in extraordinary ways but would provide them
with heightened meaning and significance. In the beginning
Alicia Thomas saw to it that Jackson-Keller would become a
community by kinship. In the end they became much more than
this—they became a community of learners and a community of
leaders.

One of Alicia Thomas's favorite thoughts on leadership is
drawn from Heider's *The Tao of Leadership* (1985, p. 15):

> The wise leader is like water. Consider water: Water
> cleanses and refreshes all creatures without distinc-
> tion and without judgment; water freely and fear-
> lessly goes deep beneath the surface of things;
> water is fluid and responsible; water follows the
> laws freely.
>
> Consider the leader: The leader works in any
> setting without complaint, without any person or
> issue that comes on the floor; the leader acts so that
> all will benefit and serves well regardless of the rate
> of pay; the leader speaks simply and honestly
> and intervenes in order to shed light and create
> harmony.
>
> From watching the movements of water, the
> leader has learned that in action, timing is every-
> thing.

> Like water, the leader is yielding. Because the
> leader does not push, the group does not resent or
> resist.

In 1988 this was a sentiment from which Mrs. Thomas derived inspiration. Today it is a sentiment that describes her new role. Is there a place in this new role for strong, direct leadership? Of course there is. Leadership is something that everyone is free to give whenever it is needed. Teachers have an obligation to lead. But principals too have an obligation to lead—to provide what is needed when it is needed. In communities, the source of authority for what leaders do gives them a new legitimacy, a new license to lead. Leadership is nothing more than serving ideas and ideals. It is nothing more than helping a community to become what it wishes to become. The burden of leadership remains on Mrs. Thomas's shoulders. But the seeds of leadership are now planted widely throughout the school, and as a result the burdens of leadership now belong to everyone.

What do principals do in schools that are becoming communities of leaders? Many things. They preach and teach, they encourage, they help, and sometimes they even yell and tell. But mostly they serve. They come to learn that the challenge of leadership in communities does not go away, it merely takes different forms—and this is the topic of the next chapter.

11

The Challenge
of Leadership

Cile Chavez, the superintendent in Littleton, Colorado, says, "My role isn't so much to make things happen but to make sense of things, to show how things fit together" (Chavez, 1992). To her, leadership is not so much doing but being. It is who she is, what she believes, and the messages she communicates to others that matter the most. Her messages of meaning encourage others to search for meaning and when this searching is shared it gives purpose and direction to the school.

Salt Creek, Illinois, superintendent Maud Hall believes that a feel for what is important, a sense of quality, a caring attitude, and a commitment to bring these to life in the school are what drive successful leaders. To her, leadership is "the ability to bring out the best in others, to motivate others to take leadership roles in the school system" (Hall, 1992). To do this, Hall believes that leaders must be able to give up power and must have low needs for personal recognition and for controlling others. Leaders devote themselves to serving the schools' purposes and to serving those who work hard to achieve these purposes.

Dallas Cristofoli, the superintendent in Howe Sound, British Columbia, believes that leadership needs to be constantly redefined and created in use as one practices. The days are long gone, she argues, when a set of patterns exist for one to follow. In today's more complex and constantly changing environment the underlying values of leaders become important determinors of what they decide and what they do. "When I look at my own decisions, there are four fundamental values that guide my considerations and actions. The first is putting the role of the student in the center of the decision making process. . . . I believe the needs of the system have often replaced the needs of the student. I always try to ask first, 'What will this do for the student?' As a corollary I ask, 'What is the student's responsibility?'" (Cristofoli, 1992, p. 12). Other values that are important to Cristofoli are: wider sharing between staff and parents and community; sharpening the focus of what is important by reviewing educational programs for relevancy; and taking personal responsibility for ensuring that the district makes sound fiscal decisions. These values, or navigational charts if you will, make it easier for her to decide and do on the spot in response to constantly changing circumstances.

To Seven Oaks (Winnipeg, Manitoba) administrator David Coulter the classroom should be the driving metaphor for organizing schools, for understanding administrative roles, and for practicing leadership. "By using the classroom as the fundamental metaphor for the organization of schooling, roles and responsibilities are seen in new ways which are more consistent with our understandings about education and children. . . . Teachers, principals and superintendents can stop seeing themselves as workers, bosses and executives and see themselves as teachers again" (1991, p. 2). Coulter and his Seven Oaks colleagues believe that replacing corporate metaphors with the classroom means relying less on borrowed theories of management and leadership and more on inventing theories and practices that better fit teaching and learning, teachers and students. The Seven Oaks team believes that the emphasis in leadership should change from management and control to stewardship and service.

This kind of leadership talk redefines what leadership is and how it should be practiced. At the heart of this talk is the importance of conceptions, values, and ideas to the practice of leadership. Sure, process skills remain important and help smooth the way. Leadership styles count too, as do good planning skills and interpersonal competence. But in this new talk leaders rely less on their people-handling skills and more on the power of compelling ideas and the meanings they hold for others.

The noted philosopher Susanne K. Langer reminded us, "Symbols and meaning make man's world far more than sensation" (1978, p. 28). And Thomas Carlyle noted, "It is in, and through symbols that man consciously or unconsciously lives, works and has meaning." Both meaning and significance are the driving forces behind our quest for connections with others and behind our quest for shared connections with common ideas and ideals. Both meaning and significance are at the heart of community building. And both meaning and significance are found as leadership becomes more idea based.

From the principal's perspective beginning the process of community building is not easy. For any number of reasons, teachers are sometimes suspicious of administrators. For any number of reasons, teachers sometimes resort to protecting themselves by distancing themselves from their work and their students. Too often, disappointing experiences in schools have resulted in tarnished visions and hurtful memories that lead teachers to seek the comfort and protection that a *gesellschaft* view of schooling can provide. Thus changing the theory from *gesellschaft* to community can be scary. Community requires the kind of involvement and commitment that, for many, might be too much of a price to pay.

One principle to keep in mind when thinking about the leadership needed to build community is that leadership itself keeps on being redefined as community builds. Principals, for example, have to think about leadership one way when they and teachers do not share the same goals and another way when goal consensus begins to emerge. And the leadership needed to help teachers get their individual psychological needs met is different from the leadership needed to create the relationship ties that bond them together into a "we." Further, as the emphasis shifts from relationship ties to idea ties leadership is redefined again.

In *Value-Added Leadership* (1990) I proposed that it might be useful for school leaders to view leadership from a "developmental perspective" and see it as comprising four stages:

1. *Bartering:* Here the principal and the teachers strike a bargain within which the principal gives to the teachers something they want in exchange for something the principal wants. The emphasis in bartering is on trading wants and needs for cooperation and compliance. This approach works best when principal and teachers do not share common goals and interests, when their stakes in the school are different.

2. *Building:* Here the principal provides the climate and interpersonal support that enhance the teachers' opportunities to fulfill individual needs for achievement, responsibility, competence, and esteem. The emphasis in building is less on trading and more on providing the conditions that enable teachers to experience psychological fulfillment. Once a minimum level of common effort has been achieved, this approach is recommended to shift the emphasis from extrinsic to intrinsic rewards.

3. *Bonding:* Here principal and teachers develop together a set of shared values about the relationships they want to share; the ties they want to create so that together they can become a community of learners and leaders, a community of colleagues. The emphasis in bonding is on relationships characterized by mutual caring and the felt interdependence that comes from mutually held obligations and commitments. This approach strives to shift the emphasis from what the principal provides to obligations and commitments teachers feel toward each other.

4. *Binding:* Here principal and teachers together commit themselves to a set of shared values and ideas that ties them together as a "we." The emphasis in binding is on developing common commitments and conceptions about purposes, about teaching and learning, and about the relationships that bring people together as a community of mind. Binding is recommended as a means to establish the moral authority that enables people to become self-managing.

In *Moral Leadership* (1992), I pointed out that leadership becomes redefined as the sources of authority for what leaders do change. Bureaucratic authority and personal authority, for example, are key in traditional conceptions of leadership that rely on bartering and building. By contrast, professional and moral authority, the sources behind bonding and binding leadership, are key to the leadership talk of Chavez, Hall, Cristofoli, and Coulter. Professional and moral authority seem also to be the driving forces behind the leadership found in Central Park East Secondary School and the Köln-Holweide Secondary School described in Chapter Three, and in the Denali Elementary School and the Jackson-Keller Elementary School described in Chapters Nine and Ten. These four sources of authority for leadership are summarized in Table 11.1.

The stages of leadership described above are not strictly developmental nor are the sources of authority outlined in Table 11.1 strictly mutually exclusive. But thinking of them as if they were can provide us with some thought frames for figuring out where to begin and for understanding how leadership needs to be redefined as community builds. For example, when "leader" and "led" are separated by different goals, when they do not trust each other, and when they do not share the same theory, the leader has to begin at the beginning. How can I get enough unity in what we are doing, enough common effort, in this school to begin a meaningful dialogue? And how can I develop at least enough trust and warmth in our relationships to sustain this dialogue?

One possibility is for the principal to begin by relying on bureaucratic authority—in the form of position power, the authority of rules, the control one has over rewards and punishments, and personal authority in the form of human relations skills—to enter into a series of trades with teachers. Rewards and punishments might be provided or withheld in exchange for minimum levels of cooperation. This is leadership by bartering. But bartering is not likely to get us very far for very long unless the emphasis changes from bureaucratic to personal authority. For this to happen, the principal will probably need to emphasize meeting people's needs (as, for example, defined by Maslow), improving the interpersonal climate in the school, build-

Table 11.1. The Sources of Authority for Leadership.

Source	Assumptions When Use of This Source Is Primary	Leadership/Supervisory Strategy	Consequences
Bureaucratic authority			
Hierarchy Rules and regulations Mandates Role expectations (Teachers comply or face consequences.)	Teachers are subordinates in a hierarchically arranged system. Supervisors are trustworthy, but subordinates are not. Goals and interests of teachers and supervisors are not the same, and supervisors must be watchful. Hierarchy equals expertise, and so supervisors know more than teachers do. External accountability works best.	"Expect and inspect" is the overarching rule. Rely on predetermined standards, to which teachers must measure up. Identify their needs and "in-service" them. Directly supervise and closely monitor the work of teachers, to ensure compliance. Figure out how to motivate them and get them to change.	With proper monitoring, teachers respond as technicians, executing predetermined scripts, and their performance is narrowed.
Personal authority			
Motivational technology Interpersonal skills Human relations Leadership (Teachers will want to comply because of the congenial climate and the rewards.)	The goals and interests of teachers and supervisors are not the same but can be bartered so that each side gets what it wants. Teachers have needs, and if they are met at work, the work gets done as required.	Develop a school climate characterized by high congeniality among teachers and between teachers and supervisors. "Expect and reward."	Teachers respond as required when rewards are available, but not otherwise; their involvement is calculated and performance is narrowed.

Table 11.1. The Sources of Authority for Leadership, Cont'd.

Source	Assumptions When Use of This Source Is Primary	Leadership/Supervisory Strategy	Consequences
	Congenial relationships and a harmonious interpersonal climate make teachers content, easier to work with, and more apt to cooperate.	"What gets rewarded gets done."	
	Supervisors must be experts in reading needs and in other people-handling skills, to barter successfully for compliance and increases in performance.	Use psychological authority in combination with bureaucratic and technical-rational authority.	
Professional authority			
Informed craft knowledge and personal expertise (Teachers respond in light of common socialization, professional values, accepted tenets of practice, and internalized expertise.)	Situations of practice are idiosyncratic, and no one best way exists.	Promote a dialogue among teachers that explicitly states professional values and accepted tenets of practice.	Teachers respond to professional norms; their practice becomes collective, they require little monitoring, and their performance is expansive.
	Scientific knowledge and professional knowledge are different, with professional knowledge created in use as teachers practice.	Translate them into professional standards.	
	The purpose of scientific knowledge is to inform, not prescribe, practice.	Give teachers as much discretion as they want and need.	

Moral authority Felt obligation and duties derived from widely shared community values, ideas, and ideals (Teachers respond to shared commitments and felt interdependence.)	Authority cannot be external but comes from the context itself and from within the teacher. Authority from context comes from training and experience. Authority from within comes from socialization and internalized values.	Require teachers to hold one another accountable for meeting practice standards. Make assistance, support, and professional development opportunities available.	Teachers respond to community values for moral reasons; their practice becomes collective, and their performance is expansive and sustained.
	Schools are professional learning communities.	Identify and make explicit the values and beliefs that define the center of the school as a community.	
	Communities are defined by their centers of shared values, beliefs, and commitments.	Translate them into informal norms that govern behavior.	
	In communities, what is considered right and good is as important as what works and what is effective; people are motivated as much by emotion and beliefs as by self-interests; and collegiality is a professional virtue.	Promote collegiality as internally felt and morally driven interdependence. Rely on the ability of community members to respond to duties and obligations. Rely on the community's informal norms to enforce professional and community values.	

Source: Adapted from Sergiovanni, 1992.

ing trust, and modeling authenticity. These are the practices of leadership by building.

The virtues that accrue from practicing leadership by building are helpful in developing community. This is the leadership that reinforces the development of a healthy sense of "I" in the school. But when leadership by building is all we have, schools still remain a collection of "I's." Developing a "we" requires stronger ties among people. Further, since in both bartering and building the connections of people to their work depend largely upon exchanging wants and needs for cooperation, they fall apart when the trading stops. Bartering and building encourage teachers and students to become involved in their work for calculated reasons.

The ties needed to develop the "we" of community come from practicing leadership by bonding and binding. Both require that the emphasis shift from bureaucratic and personal authority to professional and moral authority. Both depend upon the emergence of a community of mind—a set of shared values, ideas, and ideals that define the school as a purposeful community and teachers as a professional community.

Once a community of mind emerges, it becomes a substitute for leadership. The school becomes a place where people care for each other, help each other, devote themselves to their work, and commit themselves to a life of inquiry and learning. These ideals are central to community. They represent a norm system. And when members internalize this norm system they feel obligated to embody these ideals in their everyday lives. Motivation comes from the inside. When this happens, everyone becomes self-managing and self-leading.

In a major breakthrough, University of San Diego professor Joseph Rost offers a definition of leadership that can help to connect its practice to community building. "Leadership is an influence relationship among leaders and followers who intend real changes that reflects their mutual purposes" (1991, p. 102). This definition contains four key elements—all of which, Rost argues, must be present for relationships between and among people to be called leadership. If any one of the four is missing then these relationships might better be thought of as management or some other expression. They may have merit, they just aren't leadership. The four elements are (pp. 102–103):

1. The relationship is based on influence.
2. Leaders and followers are the people in this relationship.
3. Leaders and followers intend real change.
4. Leaders and followers develop mutual purposes.

Rost points out that conceiving of leadership as an influence relationship means that it is interactive and multidirectional. You don't have leadership if influence is just top down. Further, influence, in his definition, means the use of persuasion and not rewards and punishments or position and legal power. It is not leadership if I order, require, seduce, or threaten your compliance.

Rost also proposes that for something to be called leadership, both followers and leaders must be doing the leadership. They need not be equal in the relationship nor must everyone be leading all the time. But in any given period of time or for any given episode, both share the burdens and obligations of leadership.

Further, for leader and follower to intend real changes leadership acts must be purposeful. They must be motivated not by personal gain or by bureaucratic requirements but by a desire to better serve purposes. Finally, the purposes themselves must be shared by both leaders and followers. In the ideal they are developed together.

At first glance Rost's definition may appear too restricted. On the surface, for example, it seems to overlook the importance of symbolic leadership. In symbolic leadership the leader uses symbolic acts to communicate meanings. The principal who makes picking up trash a fetish, who works hard to ensure that student lavatories are both attractive and clean, who is passionate in removing the first signs of graffiti, and who spends Saturday mornings tending the flowers in front of the school may not qualify as a leader given Rost's definition. If by doing

these things, however, a principal is successful in communicating a belief that caring schools are attractive schools and if the
principal is successful in extending an invitation to teachers
and students to join in the burdens of making this school
attractive, then this series of acts qualifies as leadership.

Rost's definition relies on the importance of compelling
ideas and shared commitment to these ideas. Further, the roles
of followers and leaders are blurred. With shared ideas as the
source of authority, all are followers first; when anyone takes the
initiative to follow, followership becomes redefined as leadership. Leadership flourishes when leaders and followers view
each other as being credible. The stronger is this credibility the
more likely will people allow themselves to be influenced by
leadership acts, no matter what their source.

To Rost and Smith (1992, p. 199), credibility can be
thought of as encompassing five "C's": *character*, defined as honesty, trust, and integrity; *courage*, defined as the willingness to
change and to stand up for one's beliefs; *competence*, defined in
both technical and interpersonal senses; *composure*, defined as
being graceful under pressure and displaying emotion appropriately; and *caring*, defined as being concerned with the welfare
of others.

The credibility "C's" suggest that certain relationship requirements must be met before leadership can be fully and
widely expressed in a school. Not surprisingly the relationship
requirements are *gemeinschaft*. How open are we to each other?
Do we have the courage to speak, to express our true feelings, to
ask for help, to stand up for what we believe? Can we speak
knowledgeably about teaching and learning? Are we sensitive to
the views of others? Do we care about each other, our work, and
the students we serve? How do we embody this caring?

David Hagstrom and the Denali Elementary School staff
stumbled upon "The Talking Circle" as a way to help build
credibility. Hagstrom tells the story of the first-year teacher who
confronted him for not being available and supportive. This
blowup occurred while David and eleven teachers were off at a
conference together. On the spot, David and the teachers talked
about possible solutions to the problem. They came up with

several ideas: spending more time with first-year teachers individually and as a group, creating a buddy system, and so on.

As a result of this incident one of the teachers, a Native
American, taught the Denali faculty how to use the Talking
Circle. As Hagstrom (1993) describes it:

> In a talking circle all members of the community sit
> in a circle on the floor and quietly prepare a time
> for sharing. Then as the time of sharing begins, one
> person at a time holds a sacred object (for us at
> Denali, it was an eagle feather), and while we hold
> that object, we hold the floor. In other words, we
> may talk then and the others listen. There is no
> interruption. And the person must be truthful. The
> person must begin by telling of his or her lineage
> (daughter of ——, etc.). Then the person tells the
> truth of her or his concerns, joys, and wishes.
> Within our group, we decided that the focus would
> be our community. As [this teacher] informed us,
> the understanding had to be that words shared
> within our talking circle *had* to stay within our
> group. So it was that within the talking circle, mem-
> bers of our community shared their frustrations
> and their celebrations. It was all confidential. And
> in the process, we became a community.

This story brings us back to the developmental stages of
leadership. At its best, leadership by building can help create
the kind of authentic relationships among the faculty that enables them to tackle such questions as who we are and what we
want to be—the questions that ultimately bond them together
and bind them to a set of shared ideals. In communities it is the
authority of virtue not the power of position that licenses one to
lead. Virtue is embedded in what a community shares and in its
collective wisdom, a view shared by Plato.

In Plato's Utopia, the Guardians embodied virtue
through active citizenship and through relationships characterized by mutual loyalty and commitment. And among the

Guardians, leaders were required to be philosophers first. As philosophers, their orientation was *gemeinschaft* and their commitment was to how followers would fare best. This is in contrast with the stance of Machiavelli, whose intent was to prescribe how leaders become and remain successful (Kellerman, 1984)—a view with a healthy tinge of *gesellschaft*.

To Plato:

> Until. . . political greatness [leadership] and wisdom meet in one and those commoner natures who pursue either to the exclusion of the other are compelled to stand aside, cities will never have rest from their evils—no nor the human race [1956, p. 431].

To Machiavelli:

> One must be a fox in order to recognize traps, and a lion to frighten off wolves. . . . So it follows that a prudent ruler cannot, and should not, honor his word when it places him at a disadvantage. . . . If all men were good, this precept would not be good; but because men are wretched creatures who would not keep their word to you, you need not keep your word to them [1961, p. 100].

As the embodiment of virtue, Plato's Guardians were taught not only to know but to be and to be what they knew (Broudy, 1965)—a thought reminiscent of Cile Chavez's comments that opened this chapter. No one person can pull it off. Community building asks a great deal from everyone. It asks, for example, that principals, teachers, and students care for each other, learn together, inquire together, and share together in the obligations of leadership. It requires that the school become a community by kinship, of place, of mind, and of memory.

Though stewardship for the common good must be widely shared among members of a community, principals have special stewardship obligations. They must plant the seeds of community, nurture fledgling community, and protect the community once it emerges. To do this they lead by following. They lead by serving. They lead by inviting others to share in the burdens of leadership. They lead by knowing. And, like Plato's Guardians, they lead by being.

References

Albritton, M., Burns, M., Franz, D., and Tilly, D. "Alamo Heights High School and Catherine Stinson Middle School: A Study in Contrast." San Antonio, Tex.: Department of Education, Trinity University, 1991.

Barth, R. *Improving Schools from Within.* San Francisco: Jossey-Bass, 1990.

Beck, L. G. "Meeting the Challenge of the Future: The Place of a Caring Ethic in Educational Administration." *American Journal of Education*, 1992, *100*(4), 454–496.

Becker, H. *Through Values to Social Interpretation.* Durham, N.C.: Duke University Press, 1950.

Bellah, R. N., and others. *Habits of the Heart: Individualism and Commitment in American Life.* New York: HarperCollins, 1985.

Berg, N. M. "An Assessment of Student Attitudes and Perceptions of a Dropout Prevention Program at an Urban High School." Master's thesis, Department of Education, Trinity University, San Antonio, Texas, May 1992.

Blau, P. M., and Scott, W. R. *Formal Organizations.* San Francisco: Chandler, 1962.

Blumer, I. *Core Value Process.* Newton, Mass.: Newton Public Schools, 1992.

Brandt, R. "On Building Learning Communities: A Conversation with Hank Levin." *Educational Leadership*, 1992, *50*(1), 18–23.

Brendtro, L. K., Brokenleg, M., and Van Bockern, S. *Reclaiming*

Youth at Risk: Our Hope for the Future. Bloomington, Ind.: National Education Service, 1990.

Bronfenbrenner, U. "Alienation and the Four Worlds of Childhood." *Phi Delta Kappan,* 1986, *67,* 430–436.

Broudy, H. "Conflicts and Values." In R. E. Ohm and W. G. Monahan (eds.), *Educational Administration Philosophy in Action.* Norman, Okla.: University of Oklahoma, 1965.

Brown, R. G. *Schools of Thought: How the Politics of Literacy Shapes Thinking in the Classroom.* San Francisco: Jossey-Bass, 1991.

Cardellichio, T. "The Lab School: A Case Study of an Experiment in Teaching and Learning." Chappaqua, N.Y.: Robert E. Bell School, July 1992.

Carnegie Council on Adolescent Development. *Turning Points: Preparing Youth for the 21st Century.* New York: Carnegie Corporation of New York, 1989.

Center for Educational Innovation. *Clipboard.* New York: Center for Educational Innovation, publication no. 13, Summer 1992.

Central Park East Secondary School. "The Promise." School publication. New York: Central Park East Secondary School, 1988.

Chapman, R. H. Letter to parents, "Angier Greensheet." School publication. Newton, Mass.: Angier School, Nov. 18, 1991.

Chavez, C. Remarks to the Trinity Principals' Center, Trinity University, San Antonio, Tex., Sept. 30, 1992.

Close, J. J., and Wilbur, J. E. "Intercessions for Holy Family Day." *Seasonal Missalette,* Advent/Christmas, Nov. 1992–Jan. 1993, *8*(3), 79.

Cohen, D. "Families Are Struggling Against Odds to Maintain Close Bonds, Study Finds." *Education Week,* Nov. 27, 1991, p. 4.

Collins, M. N. "Making a Difference in the Classroom." Special Report, vol. 65. Grove City, Pa.: Public Policy Education Fund, Aug. 1992.

Cooley, C. H. *Social Organization.* Glencoe, Ill.: Free Press, 1956. (Originally published 1909.)

Coopersmith, S. *The Antecedents of Self-Esteem.* New York: W. H. Freeman, 1967.

Coulter, D. "The Purposes of Education." A Seven Oaks School

Division Discussion Paper. Winnipeg, Manitoba: Seven Oaks School Division No. 10, 1991.

"Creating a School Community: One Model of How It Can Be Done—An Interview with Anne Ratzki." *American Educator*, Spring 1988, pp. 10–43.

Cristofoli, D. "A New Definition of Leadership." *Snapshots: A Fax Newsletter*, Dec. 1992, 2(2), 12.

Cusick, P. *The Educational System: Its Nature and Logic.* New York: McGraw-Hill, 1992.

De Charms, R. *Personal Causation.* New York: Academic Press, 1968.

Deming, W. E. *Out of the Crisis.* Cambridge, Mass.: Center for Advanced Engineering Study, Massachusetts Institute of Technology, 1986.

Denali Elementary School. "A Collection of Thoughts to Live By." School publication. Fairbanks, Alaska: Denali Elementary School, 1991.

"Discovery Grant Proposal." School publication. Fairbanks, Alaska: Denali Elementary School, 1989.

Drucker, P. F. "The New Society of Organizations." *Harvard Business Review*, 1992, 70(1), 95–103.

Durkheim, E. *Suicide: A Study in Sociology.* (J. A. Spalding and G. Simpson, trans.) New York: Free Press, 1951. (Originally published 1897.)

Durkheim, E. *Moral Education: A Study in the Theory and Application of the Sociology of Education.* (E. K. Wilson and H. Schauver, trans.) New York: Free Press, 1961. (Originally published 1925.)

Durkheim, E. *The Division of Labor in Society.* (G. Simpson, trans.) New York: Free Press, 1964. (Originally published 1893.)

Eisner, E. "Instructional and Expressive Educational Objectives: Their Formulation and Use in Curriculum." In R. E. Stake (ed.), *Curriculum Evaluation: Instructional Objectives*, AERA monograph series. Chicago: Rand-McNally, 1969.

Eisner, E. *The Educational Imagination: On the Design and Evaluation of School Programs.* New York: Macmillan, 1979.

Erickson, E. "The Concept of Identity in Race Relations." *Daedelus*, Winter 1966, 145–171.

Etzioni, A. *The Moral Dimension*. New York: Free Press, 1988.

"Expeditionary Learning: A Design for New American Schools." A proposal to the New American Schools Development Corporation. Outward Bound USA Convenor. Greenwich, Conn., 1992.

Fischer, F. *Technocracy and the Politics of Expertise*. Newbury Park, Calif.: Sage, 1990.

Fiske, E. B. *Smart Schools, Smart Kids: Why Do Some Schools Work?* New York: Simon & Schuster, 1991.

Flinders, D. J. "Teacher Isolation and the New Reform." *Journal of Curriculum and Supervision*, 1988, *4*(1), 17–29.

Flores, A. (ed.) *Professional Ideals*. Belmont, Calif.: Wadsworth, 1988.

Flynn, G. J., and Innes, M. "The Waterloo Region Catholic School System." In R. A. Villa, J. S. Thousand, W. Stainback, and S. Stainback (eds.), *Restructuring for Caring and Effective Education*. Baltimore: Brookes, 1992.

Galtung, J. "The Basic Needs Approach." In K. Lederer (ed.), *Human Needs: A Contribution to the Current Debate*. Cambridge, Mass.: Oelgeschlager, Gunn and Hain, 1980.

Greene, D., and Lepper, M. R. "How to Turn Work into Play." *Psychology Today*, 1974, *8*(4), 49–52.

Griffin, G. "Ties That Bind: Inquiry and the Realization of Community in Schools." Holmes Group Northeast Regional Meeting, Boston, Nov. 8–9, 1991.

Hagstrom, D. "The Denali Project." In G. Smith (ed.), *Public Schools That Work: Building Community*. New York: Routledge & Kegan Paul, forthcoming.

Hagstrom, D. "The Talking Circle." Personal communication, Jan. 21, 1993.

Hall, M. "Notes from Curriculum 2000 Panel." DeKalb: Northern Illinois University, Nov. 19, 1992.

Halliburton, J. "Career Prep Perspective on Pac Rim." *Snapshots: A Fax Newsletter*, Oct.–Nov. 1992, *2*(1).

Hargreaves, A., and Tucker, E. "Teaching and Guilt: Exploring the Feelings of Teaching." A paper presented to the Seven Oaks School Division Symposium Series, Winnipeg, Manitoba, Apr. 24, 1991.

Heider, J. *The Tao of Leadership: Strategies for a New Age.* Atlanta, Ga.: Humanics Limited, 1985.

Henderson, J. G. *Reflective Teaching: Becoming an Inquiring Educator.* New York: Macmillan, 1992.

Hirsch, E. D. *Cultural Literacy: What Every American Needs to Know.* Boston: Houghton Mifflin, 1987.

Institute for Education and Transformation. *Voices from the Inside: A Report on Schooling from Inside the Classroom — Part I: Naming the Problem.* Claremont, Calif.: Claremont Graduate School, 1992.

Jackson-Keller Elementary School. "The Important Book." School publication. San Antonio, Tex.: Jackson-Keller Elementary School, 1992.

Jefferson County Public Schools/Gheens Academy. "Coalition of Essential Schools: The Conversation Continues. . . ." Spring, 1991.

Johnson, D. W., and Johnson, R. T. *Teaching Students to Be Peacemakers.* Edina, Minn.: Interaction Book Co., 1991.

Johnson, D. W., Johnson, R. T., Dudley, B., and Burnett, R. "Teaching Students to Be Peer Mediators." *Educational Leadership*, 1992, *59*(1), 10–13.

Johnson, S. M. *Teachers at Work: Achieving Success in Our Schools.* New York: Basic Books, 1990.

Kawalgy, O. "Presentation to the Summer Institute 1992." Alaska Leadership Center, Fairbanks, Aug. 3, 1992.

Kellerman, B. "Leadership as a Political Act." In B. Kellerman (ed.), *Leadership: Multidisciplinary Perspective.* Englewood Cliffs, N.J.: Prentice-Hall, 1984.

Klineburg, O. "Human Needs: A Social Psychological Approach." In K. Lederer (ed.), *Human Needs: A Contribution to the Current Debate.* Cambridge, Mass.: Oelgeschlager, Gunn and Hain, 1980.

Kunc, N. "The Need to Belong: Rediscovering Maslow's Hierarchy of Needs." In R. A. Villa, J. S. Thousand, W. Stainback, and S. Stainback (eds.), *Restructuring for Caring and Effective Education.* Baltimore: Brookes, 1992.

Langer, S. K. *Philosophy in a New Key: A Study of Symbolism in*

Reason, Rite, and Art. Cambridge, Mass.: Harvard University Press, 1978.

Lanning, S. "Denali Elementary School Study." Education 675. Fairbanks: Department of Education, University of Alaska, Fall semester, 1990.

Leakey, R., and Lewin, R. *Origins.* New York: Dutton, 1977.

Lockwood, A. T. "Central Park East Secondary School, NYC: Emphasis on Personalization." *Focus in Change,* 1990, *2*(3), 7–10.

Lortie, D. C. *Schoolteacher: A Sociological Study.* Chicago: University of Chicago Press, 1975.

MacDonald, J., and Wolfson, B. "A Case Against Behavioral Objectives." *The Elementary School Journal,* 1970, *71*(3).

Machiavelli, N. *The Prince.* Middlesex, England: Penguin, 1961.

MacIntyre, A. *After Virtue: A Study in Moral Theory.* Notre Dame, Ind.: University of Notre Dame Press, 1981.

McLaughlin, M. "Reflecting on Wingspread: District Leadership and Village Building." Unpublished paper, Stanford University, May 1992.

McPike, L., and editorial staff. "What They Do and How They Do It." *American Educator,* 1987, *12*(3), 37.

Mahoney, J. L. "Winners and Losers in the School Game." *Education Week,* Dec. 16, 1992, p. 36.

Marshall, C. "School Administrators' Values: A Focus on Atypicals." *Educational Administration Quarterly,* 1992, *28*(3), 368–386.

Maslow, A. *Motivation and Personality.* New York: HarperCollins, 1970.

Meier, D. "Success in East Harlem: How One Group of Teachers Built a School That Works." *American Educator,* 1987, *12*(3), 34–39.

Meier, D. "The Kindergarten Tradition in High School." K. Jervis and C. Montag (eds.), *Progressive Education for the 1990s: Transforming Practice.* New York: Teachers College Press, 1991.

Meier, D. "Reinventing Teaching." *Teachers College Record,* 1992, *93*(4), 594–609.

Meyer, J. "Organizations as Ideological Systems." In T. J. Sergiovanni and J. E. Corbally (eds.), *Leadership and Organizational Culture*. Urbana: University of Illinois Press, 1984.

Molina, D. D., Fish, B., and Boyle, M. "The Challenger Program: Summary of Data, First Cohort First Year Students 1990–91." San Antonio, Tex.: Trinity University, 1991.

Newton Public Schools. "Core Values of the Newton Public Schools." School publication. Newton, Mass.: Newton Public Schools, 1991.

Newton Public Schools. "Core Value Process." School publication. Newton Mass.: Newton Public Schools, 1992.

Noddings, N. "Fidelity in Teaching, Teacher Education and Research for Teaching." *Harvard Educational Review*, 1986, *56*(4), 496–510.

Noddings, N. *The Challenge to Care in Schools: An Alternative Approach to Education*. New York: Teachers College Press, 1992.

Oakes, J. "Preparing a Match: Professionalism and Effective Equitable Opportunity Structures." Seven Oaks School Division Symposium Series. Winnipeg, Manitoba, Mar. 4, 1992.

Oldenquist, A. "Community and De-alienation." In A. Oldenquist and M. Rosner (eds.), *Alienation, Community, and Work*. New York: Greenwood Press, 1991.

Ontario Ministry of Education. *Education in the Primary and Junior Divisions*. Toronto: Ontario Ministry of Education, 1975a.

Ontario Ministry of Education. *The Formative Years*. Toronto: Ontario Ministry of Education, 1975b.

Ontario Ministry of Education. *Ontario Schools Intermediate and Senior Divisions (Grades 7–12/OACs)*. (Rev. ed.) Toronto: Ontario Ministry of Education, 1989.

Orme, L., and others. "Team Teaching Takes Hold in Hatzic." *Snapshots: A Fax Newsletter*, Oct. 1992, *2*(1).

Parsons, T. *The Social System*. New York: Free Press, 1951.

Plato. "Republic." (Benjamin Jowett, trans.) In I. Edman (ed.), *The Works of Plato*. New York: Random House, 1956.

Pomeroy, D. "The Denali Project: An Interview." Fairbanks: Department of Education, University of Alaska, Nov. 11, 1992.

Rist, G. "Basic Questions About Human Needs." In K. Lederer

(ed.), *Human Needs: A Contribution to the Current Debate.* Cambridge, Mass.: Oelgeschlager, Gunn and Hain, 1980.

Rodulfo, L. "West Side School to Begin Curriculum of Understanding." *The San Antonio Light,* Sept. 10, 1992.

Rosenfeld, H. Conversation with the Trinity Partners for School Improvement and with members of the Trinity Principals' Center. Trinity University, San Antonio, Tex., Feb. 11, 1992.

Rost, J. *Leadership for the Twenty-First Century.* New York: Praeger, 1991.

Rost, J., and Smith, A. "Leadership: A Postindustrial Approach." *European Management Journal,* 1992, *10*(2), 193–201.

Rothman, R. "Study 'From Inside' Finds a Deeper Set of School Problems." *Education Week,* Dec. 2, 1992, *12*(13), 1, 9.

Rousseau, M. F. *Community: The Tie That Binds.* New York: University Press of America, 1991.

Rudnitski, R. "Through the Eyes of the Beholder: Breaking Economic, Ethnic and Racial Barriers to Parent Involvement in a School-University Partnership." San Antonio, Tex.: Department of Education, Trinity University, 1992.

Schweitzer, D. "De-alienation, Dis-anomie, and Durkheim." In A. Oldenquist and M. Rosner (eds.), *Alienation, Community, and Work.* New York: Greenwood Press, 1991.

Seeman, M. "On the Meaning of Alienation." *American Sociological Review,* 1959, *24,* 783–791.

Senge, P. M. "The Leader's New Work: Building a Learning Organization." *The Sloan Management Review,* 22(1), 1990, 7–23.

Sergiovanni, T. J. "Factors Which Affect Satisfaction and Dissatisfaction in Teaching." *Journal of Educational Administration,* 1967, *5*(2), 66–82.

Sergiovanni, T. J. *Value-Added Leadership.* Orlando, Fla.: Harcourt Brace Jovanovich, 1990.

Sergiovanni, T. J. *The Principalship: A Reflective Practice Perspective.* (2nd ed.) Needham Heights, Mass.: Allyn & Bacon, 1991.

Sergiovanni, T. J. *Moral Leadership.* San Francisco: Jossey-Bass, 1992.

Sergiovanni, T. J., and Carver, F. W. *The New School Executive: A Theory of Administration.* New York: HarperCollins, 1980.

Sergiovanni, T. J., and Starratt, R. J. *Supervision: A Redefinition.* New York: McGraw-Hill, 1993.

Sizer, T. R. *Horace's School: Redesigning the American High School.* Boston: Houghton Mifflin, 1992.

Slater, C. "Schools Called Upon to Recreate a Portion of Family Life Lost." *The San Antonio Light,* Jan. 8, 1993, 6B.

Spady, W. G. "Organizing for Results: The Basis of Authentic Restructuring and Reform." *Educational Leadership,* Oct. 1988, *47,* 4–10.

Standing Bear, L. *Land of the Spotted Eagle.* New York: Houghton Mifflin, 1933.

Starratt, R. J. "Building an Ethical School: A Theory for Practice in Educational Leadership." *Educational Administration Quarterly,* 1991, *27*(2), 185–202.

Tabor, M.B.W. "First Trying Days in the First Grade." *New York Times,* Sept. 13, 1992, p. 58.

Tönnies, F. *Gemeinschaft und Gesellschaft* [Community and Society] (C. P. Loomis, ed. and trans.) New York: HarperCollins, 1957. (Originally published 1887.)

Trice, H. M., and Beyer, J. M. "Studying Organizational Cultures Through Rites and Ceremonials." *Academy of Management Review,* 1984, *9*(4), 653–669.

Tyack, D., and Hanson, E. *Managers of Virtue: Public School Leadership in America 1820–1980.* New York: Basic Books, 1982.

Wager, B. R. "No More Suspension: Creating a Shared Ethical Culture." *Educational Leadership,* Dec. 1992, *50*(4), 34–37.

Weber, M. *The Methodology of the Social Sciences.* (E. A. Shils and H. A. Finch, trans.) New York: Free Press, 1949.

Weins, J. R. "Superintendents as Teachers: The Seven Oaks Commitment." Paper presented to the annual conference of the Canadian Association for the Study of Educational Administration, Charlottetown, Prince Edward Island, June 6, 1992.

Woods, G. H. *Schools That Work.* New York: Dutton, 1992.

Yukel, G. A. *Leadership in Organizations.* (2nd ed.) Englewood Cliffs, N.J.: Prentice-Hall, 1989.

Zwiebach, B. *The Common Life.* Philadelphia: Temple University Press, 1988.

Index

215